"This is a rich, nourishing book that
Psalm 42, drawing out gems of wisd(
tional health. In our hyper-individualize
tions can become dangerous idols that perpetuate narcissism and
self-deception. But in the context of biblical truth, they are gifts that
foster worship and knowledge of God. This book wisely recontextu-
alizes and redirects emotional awareness to the end of biblical worship. It's a timely, valuable resource for church leaders and
Christians everywhere."

> **Brett McCracken**, author, *The Wisdom Pyramid: Feeding
> Your Soul in a Post-Truth World*

"I don't speak for all leaders, but I can say from my sixty years of
living that I have days when I say, "Lord, I believe" and other days
when I say, "Lord, help me in my unbelief." It is in this ebb and flow
between satisfaction and frustration, hope and despair, feeling like
I'm on top of the world and feeling like the world is on top of me
that I find a kindred spirit in the psalmists' words. My friend, Alan
Frow, honestly and revealingly opens up the psalms to his readers
so that in our brutal honesty and in our conflicted lives we can be
formed and transformed by God's Word."

> **Dr. Barry Corey**, President of Biola University, author
> of *Love Kindness*

"I highly endorse and commend to you this valuable work by Alan
Frow. As he walks with his readers through the Psalms, he assists
them in identifying with the psalmist both in his struggles and in his
triumphs, in those moments when his faith is challenged and in
those times when he is confident in his relationship with the Lord
and in His faithfulness. In chapter after chapter he assists us in
pouring out our hearts to the Lord, and in receiving His mercy and
grace that bring deep healing to our souls."

> **Dr. Tom Sappington**, Professor at Cook School of In-
> ter-Cultural Studies and Talbot School of Theology, Au-
> thor of *Letting God be Judge*

"Alan has a remarkable way of bringing the scriptures meaningfully to bare on deep elements of the human condition. Both his friendship and his writings have been of personal help and strength to me, as we have worked through the truths unpacked in this book. Psalms for a saturated soul will reach each reader where they are and yet draw you out and into more of the life giving ways Jesus invites us each into. Recommended reading for all!"

> **Ryan Ter Mors Huizen**, Lead Pastor, Common Ground Church, Cape Town, Advance Global Team Member

"I so want to recommend Alan's new book—*Psalms for the Saturated Soul*. After two plus years of a global pandemic which has so affected how we do church and the devastating news of leadership fall outs across the global church it is no wonder that so many, especially leaders, are finding life genuinely hard to live through right now. Many feel confused, disappointed & exhausted both in how we think and feel. Where better to turn than to the Psalms? Alan brings out such timeless truths from those who have gone before us & faced all that life can throw at us. In this you will find hope and encouragement beyond your thoughts and feelings that will change you where it really matters—your very inner being, your soul."

> **Dave Holden**, Leader of New Ground Network of Churches, U.K.

"Through many a dark night of the soul, the Psalms have been my guide. I'm thankful that Alan has taken the time to point us back to those Spirit-inspired words that for countless millions have been God's means of restoring the soul."

> **Brian Broderson**, Senior Pastor, Calvary Chapel, Costa Mesa, Founder of Calvary Global Network.

"Alan masterfully analyzes our current spiritual malaise and proffers a solution. In these days where we are bombarded by a cacophony of voices solicited and unsolicited, we have to intentionally and even forcefully choose to listen to truth that will lead to our healing.

He shows us that the counsel and comfort of God are rooted in his character and person which are found in his word. In this book he shows us how to honestly and mindfully nurture the ground out of which we are growing. Alan offers us the tried and proven honest to God good word. Take, read and do for your emotional and indeed spiritual well-being.

Dr. Bulus Galadima, Catalyst for Diasporas, Lausanne Movement, Nigeria/USA

"We tend to live on either end of a polarizing emotional system—consumed with our feelings and an inability to make a change or denying our emotions altogether and living in relational deficit. If you're struggling emotionally, you're not alone. Studies and surveys continue to show that rates of anxiety and depression are moving in one direction: upward. The temptation for this generation is to make therapists the new priests or self-help the new scripture. Both can be good but neither are ultimate. Only God's timeless truth and comfort can ultimately help people of every generation, nation, language, background, and social status. Alan's book gives us permission to feel while also calling us to move with trust toward the only God who is big enough to hold all our emotions. May this book, centered on the Psalms, cut through the noise of your life to bring renewal and refreshment where you need it the most—your soul."

Nick and Kim Bogardus, Co-Founders of The Relational Group, California

"Alan's book on 'Psalms for the Saturated Soul' is one that needed to be written and it's a book that needs to be read. It needs to be read by all those whose diaries are stuffed, but whose inner lives are in famine. It needs to be read by all of us who are exhausted by the tyranny of projecting the best version of ourselves, whilst silently and slowly bleeding inwardly with discontent. Within these pages flows the liberating power and possibility of a noble re-orientation towards hope and wholeness. But before we experience this liberation, Alan presses us to audit the 'fault-lines' in our personal and collective Shalom. If your soul is like mine, you carry the wounds of foolish neglect, noisy distraction and a socialized faith. It's a faith that's perhaps too 'horizontal' and has largely drifted from joy-filled orientation around the only ultimate true north. That's the power of the Psalms and in particular Psalm 42. They overwhelmingly remind us 'where our help comes from'. They anticipate and welcome us as we are! They give us a spaciousness to celebrate, lament, pray, complain, vent and confess our sins. And all this before a God who is not disillusioned with us. He can't be, because he has no illusions about us in the first place! Alan writes like the soul coach he is, warmly and winsomely, but also humbly and persuasively. He convinces us of a timeless and compelling fresh course of saturation. He also writes like a true shepherd, reflecting the anchoring affections and assurances that Jesus, our risen Shepherd graciously offers to us. I'm confident that 'Psalms for the Saturated Soul' will meaningfully help reorientate Jesus-followers, leaders, churches and movements towards a new day of gospel humility, wholeness and vitality!"

Rigby Wallace, Founding Pastor, Common Ground Church, Cape Town, Advance Global Team M

"The world's answer to the stresses and anxieties of life is often more therapy, better management, or harder boundaries. What Alan has done with *Psalms for a Saturated Soul* is to remind the Church again of our need to commune with our Creator God through the language of the Psalms. Thank you for this gift!"

Steve Chang, Senior Pastor, Living Hope Church, Founder of SOLA Network, California

"Through the truths gained in his own courageous internal exploration, a deep fidelity to God's Word, the careful attunement to the Spirit within, and the long obedient road of pastoring others in the human condition, Alan has provided us a strong, gentle and hopeful guide to living well and faithfully with our emotional world."

Chris Williams, Marriage and Family Therapist, Renovari Counseling, California

PSALMS FOR A
SATURATED SOUL

An Ancient Guide to Emotional Health

Alan Frow

Psalms for a Saturated Soul: An Ancient Guide to Emotional Health

Copyright ©2022 by Alan Peter Frow

Imprint: Independently published in coordination with Advance Publishing

Content Editor: Will Anderson

Cover Design: Becki Cox

Editor: Kristine Nethers

Layout: Jon Marshall

ISBN: 9798803317210

I dedicate this book to Peter and Jill Frow, Chris Williams, Bill Gaultiere, Nick and Kim Bogardus, Tom and Katy Sappington. These wise physicians of the soul have helped me to see how through God's grace, emotions can be both mentionable and manageable.

CONTENTS

FOREWARD

Everyday I pray from the Psalms. Many I've memorized and some of these I sing—whether I feel like it or not. The Psalms are a lifeline for me.

The Psalms are the soul book of the Bible. They give us the language for what we're feeling and how to pray our emotions with faith in God: complaints and gratitudes, praises and laments, desperate petitions and bold faith, faithful friendship and betrayal, angry curses and quiet selahs, universal human experiences and prophecies of the Christ—all this and more are here for us.

In the ministry of Soul Shepherding that I lead, we talk with pastors, missionaries, and church leaders everyday—the biggest-hearted and brightest people on earth! Yet, more than ever in my thirty years of ministry, I see that the souls of Jesus' leaders and people are worn out and weighed down by the troubles in our world and conflicts in our communities.

Today it's urgent for Christ-followers to gather together and open the Psalms to help us pray, worship, and nourish our souls in God alone.

In Psalms for a Saturated Soul my friend Alan Frow opens up Psalm 42 for our thirsty souls. This psalm is one of my favorites, which I've sung devotionally countless times and used in various teachings. Yet, I gleaned many new gems for my life and ministry from the Lord through Alan's writing.

By reflecting on and praying Psalm 42 with Alan, we can learn how to walk the path of life that's in all the Psalms, growing in emotional health and spiritual vitality together:

As the deer pants for streams of water so my soul longs for you, O God . . .

In love the Spirit of Jesus is wooing us into God's presence. To respond with longing for God is the breath of life for our souls.

I pour out my soul . . .

To be filled with Holy Spirit I need to pour out my soul to God, as the Psalmist shows us. I need to release my anxiety, shame, and anger. I need to grieve my sins, wounds, and weaknesses.

Why, O my soul, are you downcast with me? . . .

The Lord Jesus, with his Father and Spirit, listen to our souls—we need to join them. We need to hear the feelings below the surface of our lives and verbalize them to God and to one another in friendship and as we co-labor to share Jesus' gospel in our world.

Put your hope in God, for I will yet praise Him . . .

We also need to talk to our souls. We need to speak the grace and truth of God's word into our feelings, thoughts, and whole being.

Deep calls to deep in the roar of you waterfalls . . . His steadfast love is with me . . .

Alan writes that we only get to the refreshment of the waterfalls of God's love by following the poetry and progression of this prayer.

Let's get drenched in Holy Spirit waterfalls!

I know Alan personally and I've seen how he lives into the psalmist's life of emotional honesty, love for others, and courageous faith in God. It's a blessing to have him guide us devotionally verse-by-verse, that our souls might be encouraged and strengthened in the Lord, so we can love people for Jesus' sake with great joy.

Bill Gaultiere, Ph.D.
Founder, Psychologist & Spiritual Director
Soul Shepherding
Author of *Journey of the Soul*
Irvine, CA

INTRODUCTION:
A PERPLEXING PARADOX

When I get honest, I admit I am a bundle of paradoxes. I believe and I doubt, I hope and get discouraged, I love and I hate, I feel bad about feeling good, I feel guilty about not feeling guilty. I am trusting and suspicious. I am honest and I still play games. Aristotle said I am a rational animal; I say I am an angel with an incredible capacity for beer.

Brennan Manning, *The Ragamuffin Gospel*[1]

Maybe, like me, you're a bundle of paradoxes.

On one hand, I bear God's image. I have a marvelous capacity to cultivate beauty, experience intimacy, invent solutions, make promises, show mercy, resist evil, build culture,

---

[1]Brennan Manning, *The Ragamuffin Gospel* (United States: Multnomah Books, 2015), 11.

and encounter wonder. On my best days, God's glory is profoundly displayed in my life. Humans can be quite magnificent, really — just a little lower than the angels.

On the other hand, I have this inescapable sense that I don't reflect God as I should. The mirror of my life gets smudged and tarnished. I have a dreadful capacity to corrupt beauty, shatter intimacy, create problems, break promises, exploit the vulnerable, be tempted by evil, destroy culture, and become jaded with wonder. Humans can be quite awful, really — just a little higher than the devils.

There is a fickle fragility in my soul. I flit back and forth between peace and anxiety, joy and sorrow, obedience and disobedience, forgiveness and bitterness. Like termites in a wooden boat, my inconsistencies gnaw holes in my soul—then as I frantically bail water to remain buoyant, discouragement gushes over me. Can you relate?

What do we do about the frustrating duality of our souls? Proposed solutions abound.

Moralism says effort is the solution. If we can be good enough — through religion or neighborliness or parenting or profession — our positive behavior will outweigh our bad behavior. But this places an oppressive burden to perform that's easily squashed by our next mess-up (which is likely imminent).

Mysticism says contemplation is the solution. But meditation isn't medication, and sometimes silence makes our failures scream louder. Mindfulness plus good Karma minus bad Feng Shui does not equal zen.

Psychology says that healing from trauma inflicted by others is the solution. This is immensely important and can be instrumental in helping someone heal. It has certainly helped me. But secular psychotherapy has no category for the biblical doctrine of sin, which scripture names as the *greatest* threat to human flourishing. As Dietrich Bonhoeffer writes:

> *The most experienced psychologist or observer of human nature knows infinitely less of the human heart than the simplest Christian who lives beneath the Cross of Jesus. The greatest psychological insight, ability, and experience cannot grasp this one thing: what sin is. Worldly wisdom knows what distress and weakness and failure are, but it does not know the godlessness of man. And so it also does not know that man is destroyed only by his sin and can be healed only by forgiveness. Only the Christian knows this. In the presence of a psychiatrist*

*I can only be a sick man; in the presence of a Christian brother
I can dare to be a sinner.*[2]

Individualism posits "being yourself" as the solution, as
Polonius advises Hamlet: "To thine own self be true."[3] If
nothing else, this mantra exasperates our sense of duality.
Much of the time, we're unsure of who we are or who we
want to be. In response, individualism sometimes celebrates
the paradox within, blurring the lines between right and
wrong. But impropriety leads to insecurity, leaving us with
the burning question: *To which self should I be true?*

THE PSALMS: FORMATION NOT FORMULA

Enter the Psalms — the hymnbook of God's people.
The Psalms don't offer simple formulas to solve the paradox
of our souls. Instead, they employ the language of formation.
They give us permission to be in flux, while simultaneously
pointing us to the unchanging stability of our Creator. The
Psalms let us rant and weep, sing and scream, laugh and la-

---

[2] Dietrich Bonhoeffer, *Life Together and Prayerbook of the Bible* (vol. 5 of
Dietrich Bonhoeffer Works; Minneapolis: Fortress Press, 1996), 115.

[3] William Shakespeare, *Hamlet, The Prince of Denmark,* Open Source
Shakespeare (United States: George Mason University, 2003), 1.3.565,
https://www.opensourceshakespeare.org/views/plays/play_view.php
?Act=1&Scene=3&Scope=scene&WorkID=hamlet.

ment — all with an eye to heaven, knowing that our help comes from the Lord (Ps. 121:1). As a trellis prods a vine sunward, so the Psalms turn our souls God-ward. In real life, confusion and confidence often go hand-in-hand, thus the Psalms speak powerfully to the intricate anatomy of our souls.

As you read the Psalms, it's immediately obvious that God doesn't want his people to pretend. The God of the Bible wants his people to be brutally honest with themselves and with him. He's not interested in platitudes or pseudo-peace. Religious charades might fool others, even ourselves at times, but God sees our souls as they truly are.

SOULS OF THE SAINTS

In the modern world, we often think of the soul as the immaterial part of you that flies off to heaven when you die. But in biblical theology, your soul (Hebrew: nephesh) is your whole person, including your will, mind, emotions, and body. Thus the Psalms speak directly to our souls, expressing the vast breadth of human experience, as Calvin notes:

I have been wont to call this book not inappropriately, "An Anatomy of all Parts of the Soul;" for there is not an emotion of which any one can be conscious that is not here represented as in a mirror.[4]

When reading the Psalms, we discover we're not alone. We suddenly realize, with a sigh of relief, that the path we're on is well-worn by the saints before us. Our bloodied knees don't make us freaks; they merely signal we're on the path of formation. Satan would have us believe that, because we struggle, we're unworthy of Christian fellowship. The Psalms retort: No, these are the normal growing pains of a child of God.

Walter Brueggemann says that when we read the Psalms, the experience of the psalmist interacts with our own experience:

> *The work of prayer is to bring these two realities together — the boldness of the Psalms and the extremities of our experience — to let them interact, play with each other, and illuminate each other.*[5]

---

[4]John Calvin, *Commentary on the Book of Psalms, Vol. 1,* translated by James Anderson, (Grand Rapids: Christian Classics Ethereal Library) https://www.ccel.org/ccel/calvin/calcom08/calcom08.i.html.

[5]Walter Brueggemann, *Praying the Psalms: Engaging Scripture and the Life of the Spirit,* (United States: Cascade Books, 2007), 23.

In other words, we don't just read the Psalms; they read us. They unlock the prayers, petitions, and laments of other faith sojourners, revealing the sacred solidarity of saints from every age. They have found God to be both present and good, even when their souls were disoriented or faint. They testify that indeed there is hope for you and I, because God is good and ever-present.

A COMMUNITY OF SOULS

The church is a community of souls, therefore it's not only about individual health, but the collective health of the entire bride of Christ. The church I lead and the family of churches I am a part of are not as fluent as we should be in the language of the soul, and it has hurt us. We are fairly fluent in the language of Christology, ecclesiology and missiology. But there is a hesitancy around psychology and sociology because they can be so subjective. "Let's stick to gospel truth," we tend to say. But in protecting the gospel (which is right), we've neglected how it applies to soul care. After all, Christ is the great physician who gives rest to our souls (Mt 11:28).

The past year has provided a rude awakening about the consequences of neglecting communal soul health. In November 2021, I sat with six other leaders from our church network. There was a furrow-browed sobriety around the table that day. Two of our dear friends and leaders in our movement had just stepped down, in part, due to patterns of emotional and relational unhealth. Though relieved we had escaped the spectacular moral scandals so prevalent in the headlines these days, we were nonetheless heartbroken. How did we get here?

We felt blindsided by a threat we didn't know existed. Like the quiet-footed foxes ruining the vineyard in Song of Solomon, emotional unhealth had covertly crept into our leadership team. We didn't notice until it was too late. We often do wolf-checks, but rarely fox-checks. Foxes seem less destructive than wolves, but left to their own devices, they're just as deadly. Maybe we looked the other way because of the giftedness of these leaders. Fruitfulness can cover a multitude of foxes. Until it doesn't.

In the past ten years, we've seen the gospel advance in encouraging ways through our network, yet we concluded around that table that Jesus was using this crisis to lead us away from hubris towards humility, away from a self-confident swagger toward a God-reliant limp. We resolved to self-audit our souls more seriously and to build a sturdier culture of accountability. With sage-like wisdom, my friend Rigby Wallace articulated our conviction: "In this next season together, the gospel must advance along two frontiers: to the outermost parts of our world and to the innermost parts of our souls."

The writing of this book was commissioned out of that conversation. This isn't for church leaders only; it's for anyone who longs for their soul to thrive, not merely survive (3 Jn 2). This book is for those who believe the gospel impacts all of life — the Savior who forgives sins is also the Good Shepherd who restores souls. This book is for those whose unstable emotions ache for the commanding calm of Jesus' words and Spirit. This book is born out of some teaching I've done from the psalms, but more importantly, it's a book born out of God's work in me. Into my paradox, he continues to bring peace.

May the gospel advance not only to the outermost parts of our world, but also to the innermost parts of our souls.

PSALM 42

TO THE CHOIRMASTER. A MASKIL OF THE SONS OF KORAH.

As a deer pants for flowing streams, so pants my soul for you,
O God. My soul thirsts for God, for the living God.
When shall I come and appear before God?
My tears have been my food day and night,
while they say to me all the day long,
  "Where is your God?"

These things I remember as I pour out my soul:
how I would go with the throng and lead them in procession to
the house of God with glad shouts and songs of praise, a
multitude keeping festival.

Why are you cast down, O my soul,
and why are you in turmoil within me? Hope in God; for I
shall again praise him, my salvation and my God.

My soul is cast down within me; therefore I remember you from
the land of Jordan and of Hermon, from Mount Mizar. Deep
calls to deep at the roar of your waterfalls;
all your breakers and your waves have gone over me.
By day the LORD commands his steadfast love, and at night
his song is with me, a prayer to the God of my life.

I say to God, my rock: "Why have you forgotten me?
Why do I go about mourning because of the oppression of the
enemy?" As with a deadly wound in my bones,
my adversaries taunt me,
while they say to me all the day long, "Where is your God?"
Why are you cast down, O my soul,
and why are you in turmoil within me? Hope in God; for I
shall again praise him, my salvation and my God.

CHAPTER 1:

THE SATURATED SOUL

Why, my soul, are you downcast? Why so disturbed within me?
Psalm 42:5a

Burn-out. Exhaustion. Workaholism. Those are a few symptoms of my generation — a generation that spent the 80's and 90's addicted to Prozac, donning power suits with shoulder pads, and launching multi-million dollar tech startups from their parents' garages. Yuppie flu (a euphemism for chronic fatigue) infected us with pandemic-like potency.

Naively, we wore burn-out a bit like a badge of honor. The cool kids lived at work and lived to work. Everybody was red-lining on reserve, burning the midnight oil, chasing the next deal. Business was booming. Revenue was up. But emotional and physical health was in the gutter.

Today, work-life balance is a treasured topic, and I'm grateful for that. I'm also encouraged that churches are reemphasizing a theology of sabbath, because of course, burn-out is still prevalent. But it's not the hot topic it was 25 years ago. Today, our lives are not stretched thin as much as they're weighed down.

SO FULL, WE'RE EMPTY

Sometimes we're thirsty because we're too full of the wrong things. You can eat loads of salty popcorn until you're stuffed, but all that sodium will make you unbearably thirsty. In the same way, our souls can be so intoxicated with things other than God that they need detoxing before we can drink from God's river of life. This is what I call a *saturated soul* and I believe it is a cultural pandemic.

Our souls are saturated with nonstop news cycles that bombard us with calamities around the clock and around the globe. Our souls, designed by God to empathize with the hurting, are burdened beyond what they can bear. It's little wonder we feel numb. The circuit breaker of our souls trips. We shut off to survive. Callousness isn't our goal — it's a survival tactic.

Our souls are saturated with entertainment. Endless streaming services claw for our attention and wallets. When one episode ends, within seconds another starts automatically. Binging is touted as "taking a break," but really it's breaking us. The title of Neil Postman's 1985 classic, *Amusing Ourselves to Death*, proved to be prophetic.

Our souls are saturated with online connectivity — a slew of mile-wide, inch-deep acquaintances replace the deep, embodied intimacy our souls crave. We try to be known using platforms that isolate us. Rather than friends around the table, looking each other in the eyes, we're loners peering into the glow of screens.

This world offers a feast of technology and information, but ironically, the more we gorge ourselves, the more hungry we become. Oversaturation promises satisfaction while slowly starving us. Could it be that we've fire-hosed our souls into an emotional drought?

I find this paradox at work in my own life in perplexing ways. God alone can satisfy the human soul, as Augustine writes: "Almighty God, You have made us for Yourself and our hearts are restless until they find their rest in You."[6] I have experienced such deep satisfaction and comfort from God's presence in my soul.

But sadly, like the well-known hymn, I'm prone to wander from the God I love. While my soul thirsts for the living water of Christ, I still stoop to drink from the bitter waters of Marah. C.S. Lewis sums up humanity's disallegiance well: "Human history is the long and terrible story of man trying to find something other than God which will make him happy."[7] The Old Testament prophet Jeremiah warned Israel about the dangers of seeking life outside the Lord:

> *For my people have committed two evils:*
> *they have forsaken me,*
> *the fountain of living waters,*
> *and hewed out cisterns for themselves,*
> *broken cisterns that can hold no water.*

Jeremiah 2:13

I can be a real sucker for broken cisterns, how about you? Broken cisterns not only let precious water leak out, but they also let dirt in, which contaminates any water that's been

---

[6]Augustine of Hippo, *Confessions*, Book I, Chapter 1.

[7] C.S. Lewis, *Mere Christianity* (New York: Macmillan, 1952), 53-54.

conserved. But these self-made cisterns leave us feeling over-fed-yet-underfed, gorged yet grasping, filled but famished.

A PSALM FOR THE SATURATED SOUL

In Psalm 42, we meet someone caught in this same dilemma — thirsty for God's presence but oversaturated with the things of the world. In the first verse of the psalm, he expresses the dryness of his soul and his longing to be quenched by God's presence:

As the deer pants for streams of water,
so my soul pants for you, my God.
My soul thirsts for God, for the living God.

Yet, despite his thirst the psalmist's soul is also overflowing with turmoil. Verse four says: 'These things I remember as I pour out my soul." In order to drink in God's presence, he must first pour out his soul. Psalm 42 is not a quick-fix formula for our thirsty souls. It points to a process of emptying, investigating, reconnecting and speaking to our souls in the hope of God's promise to refresh us more fully than we ever dared dream. Like the psalmist, to fill our souls with God we must first empty our souls of all else.

TOO FULL TO FEEL

One of the dynamics of the saturated soul is that we are too full to feel. Like a child scribbling too many colors on a page, the barrage of emotions in ourselves and others clash on the canvas of our souls, and the end product is the dull gray of numbness.

If you're like me, you know the wretched feeling of wanting to feel, but being unable to. You sit listening to someone you love tell you an amazing story of answered prayer. You celebrate with them cerebrally, but not emotionally. You watch another devastating crisis on the news and you feel unable to empathize. Like the Rascal Flatts song, you "feel bad that you don't feel bad,"[8] or at least not as bad as you think you *should* feel. You know that it's right to rejoice with those who rejoice and weep with those who weep, but it feels forced. You listen to a powerful sermon or song, knowing you should embrace the wonder of it, but instead you feel indifferent. The guilt of not feeling is almost worse than the numbness itself.

---

[8] Rascal Flatts, "I Feel Bad," Genius, accessed April 4, 2022, https://genius.com/Rascal-flatts-i-feel-bad-lyrics.

We get so desperate to feel again, we'll actually harm our-selves to revive our emotions. Pink Floyd's 1979 hit, "Com-fortably Numb", [9] describes fighting numbness with narcotics:

> *There is no pain, you are receding*
> *A distant ship smoke on the horizon*
> *I have become comfortably numb...*
> *Just a little pinprick*
> *There'll be no more, ah*
> *But you may feel a little sick.*
> *I have become comfortably numb.*

Others fight numbness by self-injury. The Mayo Clinic explains the rationale of cutting or burning oneself: "People so badly want to feel something when they are otherwise dis-sociated and numb." [10] Feeling pain becomes better than feeling nothing. But mutilating your flesh doesn't solve the problem in your soul. Like narcotics, they offer temporary relief, followed by painful emotions like guilt and shame.

---

[9] Pink Floyd, "Comfortably Numb" Genius, accessed April 4, 2022, https://genius.com/Pink-floyd-comfortably-numb-lyrics.

[10] "Self-Injury/ Cutting," *Mayo Clinic*, Dec. 7, 2018, https://www.mayoclinic.org/ diseases-conditions/self-injury/ symptoms-causes/syc-20350950

They push people into a life of secrecy and denial. No doubt, self-injury is one of the saddest symptoms of a saturated soul.

FREEDOM TO FEEL

Still others normalize numbness, as if it's a virtue. We justify our stoicism with various mantras: "I'm too strong to feel," or "I'm too grounded in Christ to let emotions push me around." There's certainly validity to emotional resilience, but many of us who grew up in the church were taught to ostracize our feelings in unhealthy ways.

As a teenager, my father sat with me at the kitchen table and drew a picture of a steam train pulling some carriages. On the train he wrote the word "Bible" and on the carriages he wrote the words "feelings." The message was: Let God's Word lead and your feelings follow, not the other way around. It was wise counsel for an emotionally stormy young man, and thanks to my Dad, I've learned to ground my fickle feelings on the unshakable foundation of God's Word. Emotions are a wicked master if we're slaves to them.

But emotions are also a profound gift from God, and too often my pendulum swings toward emotional denial. I'm unduly suspicious of my feelings. I'm stoic where I should be soft-hearted. Honestly, really happy people tend to annoy me and really sad people tend to exhaust me. More concerningly, my stoicism distances me from Jesus himself, who scripture calls a "man of sorrows, acquainted with suffering" (Is 53:3), and also "a man anointed with joy above his fellows" (Heb 1:9). If Jesus sounds too emotional to me, something's wrong.

Rather than check our emotions at the door, we're to use them for God's glory. It's noteworthy that the fruit of the Spirit in Galatians 5 have an emotional dimension: love, joy, peace, patience, kindness, goodness, faithfulness, self-control (Gal 5:22). The Spirit-filled person is an emotionally healthy person. The incarnation, in which Christ exercised the full range of human emotion, proves that we're *meant* to feel. God's love isn't just his willpower, exercised impassionately through gritted teeth; it's his affection and passion.

Christ gives us freedom to feel *fully*, and wisdom to feel *rightly*. He teaches us to pull negative emotions out from under the rug, into the open, where we can process them in a safe environment of grace. In the next chapter, I'll unpack how to do that, using Psalm 42 as our guide.

CHAPTER 2:
POUR OUT YOUR SOUL (PART 1)

My tears have been my food day and night, while they say to me all day long, 'Where is your God? "These things I remember as I pour out my soul, how I would go with the throng and lead them in procession to the house of God with glad shouts and songs of praise, a multitude keeping festival."

Psalm 42:3-4

So, we have established that the Psalmist has a saturated soul. He is too full to feel.

How does he process his soul from emotional saturation to emotional health? Essentially, he *pours out his soul* to God.

What does this practice mean? Is it possible to reduce it to some formational rhythms? At face value, pouring out our souls means letting go of what our souls are not meant to hold. After a vacation season of unhealthy eating, we often detox by drinking plenty of water, eating high fiber foods, and cutting calories. We take supplements that cleanse our livers and reduce inflammation in our joints. Imagine if we could recognize seasons that were toxic for our souls as easily as we recognized seasons that were toxic for our bodies! What if we were as deliberate with our soul cleanses as we are with our diet cleanses?

In this chapter we will explore what it means to pour out, or *detox* our souls, through the practice of lament.

LEARNING TO LAMENT

Few locations capture the idea of lament like the Wailing Wall in Israel. I used to be saddened by the idea of the Wailing Wall. My parents lived on a *kibbutz* for a period early on in their marriage and made frequent visits back to Israel over the years, so I heard their stories about men and women dressed in black, placing prayers on pieces of paper in the cracks of the wall, rocking back and forth in prayer with gut-wrenching cries. It was somewhat depressing to me.

My parents recently told me two things about the Wailing Wall that have stuck with me. The first is that Jewish people lament the fact that they can no longer access the temple. The door to the Temple Mount, just yards from the Wailing Wall, is closed to Jews and Christians since it's now been turned into a Mosque. Thus, the Wailing Wall is the only formal place for Jews to gather and pray to *Yahweh* in Jerusalem. The second thing my parents told me is that Jews see the Wailing Wall as a place where Gentiles are welcome to pray. Apparently, this is because when King Solomon dedicated the temple to God in the Old Testament, he prayed that foreigners would be welcomed.

> *As for the foreigner who does not belong to your people Israel but has come from a distant land because of your name— for they will hear of your great name and your mighty hand and your outstretched arm—when they come and pray toward this temple, then hear from heaven, your dwelling place*
> 2 Kings 8:41-43

So, the Wailing Wall signifies God's hospitality toward both Jews and Gentiles. For centuries, God's people have come from near and far to pour out their souls before the God who hears from heaven. It's a tangible symbol that God not only gives permission to grieve, but he actually prioritizes it. So, the longer I live, the more I long to visit the Wailing Wall with my own tears and paper prayers.

This is what we see taking place in Psalm 42:4. "My tears have been my food day and night, while they say to me all day long, 'Where is your God?'"

Consider the intensity of the psalmist's sorrow. He's been crying constantly, probably ugly-crying, day and night. He has insomnia. His face is all puffy. His nose is red and swollen. His beard is unkempt, encrusted with mucus and tears. He's lost his appetite. Even if some of the psalmist's language is hyperbolic, he's more than a little choked up — he's totally disoriented.

Old Testament scholar, Walter Brueggemann, has developed a helpful way of categorizing the Psalms, which includes the disorientation of Psalm 42.[11] He suggests we regularly find our souls in one of three places:

1. Orientation: a place where everything makes sense in our lives

2. Disorientation: a place where we've sunk into the pit

3. Reorientation: a place where we realize God has lifted us out of the pit and into a new place of gratitude and awareness about our lives and God

Not surprisingly, Brueggemman places Psalm 42 in the disorientation category because it expresses anger, confusion

---

[11] Brueggemann, *Praying the Psalms,* 2.

and a sense of God's absence. The biblical term for pouring out our soul when we feel disorientated is *lament*. We need a category for biblical lament in our lives, not as a destination, but as a layover on the way to reorientation. A whole book of the Bible is dedicated to lament (Lamentations), and over one third of the Psalms fit into this category. God dignifies seasons of disorientation and gives us a way to worship Him in these seasons through lament. Henri Nouwen writes, "I have found that much of prayer is grieving."[12]

Andrew Peterson's call-and-response worship song, "Is He Worthy?"[13], artfully demonstrates what it looks like to wrestle with disorientation even while striving to orient our hope in Christ:

> *Do you feel the world is broken? (We do)*
> *Do you feel the shadows deepen? (We do)*
> *But do you know that all the dark won't*
> *Stop the light from getting through? (We do)*
> *Do you wish that you could see it all made new? (We do)*
> *Is all creation groaning? (It is)*
> *Is a new creation coming? (It is)*
> *Is the glory of the Lord to be the light within our midst? (It is)*

---

[12]Henri J. M Nouwen, *The Return of the Prodigal Son: A Story of Homecoming* (United States: Crown Publishing Group, 2013) 237.

[13] Andrew Peterson, *"Is He Worthy?"* Genius, accessed March 10, 2002, https://genius.com/Andrew-peterson-is-he-worthy-lyrics.

Is it good that we remind ourselves of this? (It is)

Depending on your age, tradition and disposition you may feel more or less comfort with the idea of lament. Maybe you fear that complaining to God will arouse his disapproval or expose your lack of faith. You might come from a more stoic faith tradition that taught you a stiff upper lip approach to disorientation. Or you might come from a "word of faith" tradition that taught you to suppress lament in order to embrace positivity. Many men grew up hearing from fathers and coaches that "cowboys don't cry." I've found it helpful to remember that lament is essentially crying to God, and when I look at how much David and Jesus cried, I'm comforted and challenged.

LAMENT LIKE DAVID

If we do a study on crying in the Psalms, we find that God not only tolerates tears — he treasures them. We see this especially in the psalms of Israel's most famous king, David, who had a heart like God's heart. In Psalm 6:2, David's soul is so troubled that he writes:

> *Be gracious to me oh God, for I am languishing;*
> *heal me, O LORD, for my bones are troubled.*

Here is David, the courageous warrior-poet, *languishing*. Can't he just pull himself together? Can't he just go down to the river and sling a few stones? Can't he just pick up his harp and sing a joyful song? Apparently not. In verse 6, his anguish continues: "I am weary with my moaning, every night I flood my bed with tears; I drench my couch with my weeping." In Hebrew, this verse literally says: "I am swimming in a bed of tears!" As much as I'd love to point out other Psalms that teach us to rejoice in the midst of sorrow, I will restrain myself. We will get to them later. For now, let's sit in this one for a minute. In this psalm, David can't seem to snap out of his weeping. Still, his confidence in God is not defeated: "The Lord has heard my plea. The Lord accepts my plea."

Likewise, in Psalm 56:8, David describes God as a collector of our tears and a recorder of our sorrows.

> *You keep track of all my sorrows.*
> *You have collected all my tears in your bottle.*
> *You have recorded each one in your book.*

Weeping is not a sign of God's absence but of his presence. God collects every tear we cry in a bottle, records every one of our sorrows, and keeps track of them in a book. He is described as a tender soul physician, skillfully examining his patient to track every sign of their anguish. God's attention to detail is remarkable: He's so attentive to us in order to restore our souls, as David affirms at the end of the psalm:

> *For you have delivered my soul from death, yes, my feet from falling, that I may walk before God in the light of life.*
> Psalm 56:13

My close friends affectionately tease me that my bladder is "right behind my eyes." It's a fun way of saying that I cry easily. It's true. For some reason, especially when I talk about Jesus, I tear up. I blame my dad, who tends to do the same. I can't turn on my tears at will, thank goodness, but I have learned the art of talking through my tears. But the older I get, the less I cry. Maybe it's because a few decades of leadership has taught me how tears can be used inappropriately to manipulate people. I've had to learn to be strong for my family and church, which has meant crying less — although, from time to time, we *all* need a good cry.

Every morning I sit in an old leather chair in the corner of our lounge with my coffee and Bible. From the chair, I look out of two large picture windows with panoramic views of our yard, and the mature trees beyond our wooden fence.

I can also see my wife, who usually spends her mornings on our porch. One morning, about a year into the pandemic, I sat in my usual spot, but on this particular morning our daughter was sleeping on a couch to my right in the TV room. Something had happened the night before that caused her to want to sleep there. She had been *languishing* in a very sad place for some months — a sadness created by isolating pandemic regulations, disappointment with a leader in her youth group, and some poor choices she made to try and cope with her pain.

The night before, she had reluctantly joined us at the church's monthly prayer gathering. During worship, God began to meet with her in a way that made her sob uncontrollably. We had never seen her respond to God's presence like this. She ran out of the meeting and returned some time later red-eyed. My wife and I tried to comfort her. Once we got home she asked us, "Can you tell me what God's voice is like? I think he spoke to me."

Both mystified and thrilled, we enquired, "What do you think He said?"

"He said that he forgives me and has work for me to do for Him in England," she replied.

"Sounds like God," remarked my wife.

That night our daughter felt the sadness beginning to subside, but didn't want to sleep in her room because it felt dark to her, so she crashed on our sleeper couch.

As I watched her sleep that morning, I thanked God for His kindness, marveled at the weight of leading a family and church through a pandemic, and I began to sob. I cried in a way I had not wept for in ten years. My sobs were so loud, they woke my daughter up. My son heard them from his bedroom and came running in. My wife heard them from the porch, and thinking someone had died, came running to comfort me.

Through tears, I reassured my wide-eyed family: "Don't worry, it's a good cry. I'm happy, but the last year has been so hard." My wife, wise as ever, gave our children a quick lesson on the goodness of tears.

"Dad has had to be strong for us and the church," she said. "He has absorbed a lot of people's pain this year. These tears are tears of relief about a season changing. There's no shame in crying. In fact, tears are God's gift." That morning I lamented. I cried tears of sadness and relief. And God was near.

I am not saying you should force tears. But it is important that you let yourself cry. Do not avoid lament, as if it's a lack of faith. In reality, it's really God's way to a more authentic faith. Don't wallow in self-pity, but give yourself permission (as God does) to lament.

LAMENT LIKE JESUS

Tears are one of the first ways that we begin to empty our saturated souls so that they can be filled again with God. Perhaps you're familiar with the shortest verse in the Bible: "Jesus wept" (Jn 11:35). Jesus wept for his dead friend Lazarus before he raised him from the dead. The word "wept" here means "to snort like a horse." Jesus ugly-cried for his friend, showing that in his full humanity, he felt the sting of death and loss. Jesus also wept over Jerusalem as he lamented their hard hearts and the looming devastation awaiting that city. Hebrews 5:7 describes Jesus' prayer life as one of lament:

In the days of his flesh, Jesus offered up prayers and supplications, with loud cries and tears, to him who was able to save him from death, and he was heard because of his reverence.

While this verse refers to Jesus' prayer life generally, it probably refers specifically to the Garden of Gethsemane. In the Garden, Jesus was so troubled he sweated drops of blood. Jesus didn't throw a tantrum to get his own way; rather, He cried, "Father, if it is possible let this cup of suffering be taken from me. Yet, not my will but yours be done" (Mat. 26:39 NLT). There was no ounce of manipulation in his words. His tears flowed from a place of reverence as he wrestled to submit to His Father's will. That is why God heard him (Heb 5:7). And God answered, 'No, my Son, this cup cannot be taken from you." Jesus' reverent tears were not only acceptable to God: they were precious to God. The Son was willing to be alienated from His Father so that we might draw near to the Father.

Thanks to Christ's sacrifice we can now cry out to our Father, and like the tears of Jesus in the Garden, God will hear us in our darkest hour. The Father's absence from Jesus in his darkest hour means God's presence will be with us in ours. Even when we lament. *Especially* when we lament.

CHAPTER 3:

POUR OUT YOUR SOUL (PART 2)

These things I remember as I pour out my soul, how I would go with the throng and lead them in procession to the house of God with glad shouts and songs of praise, a multitude keeping festival.

Psalm 42:4

CONFESSION

We're talking about ways in which we pour out the toxins in our souls so that they may be filled with God again. One of the ways the psalmist does this is confession. He remembers a time when he was at the front of the procession, eager to get to the house of God. Though he's still fulfilling his worship leading role (he is writing a psalm after all) he seems to be dragging his feet to the house of God. He no longer leads the procession of pilgrims to the temple. He's lost touch with both the presence of God. Whatever the case, few things are worse than a demoralized worship leader, caught in the gap between ministry responsibility and devotional dullness. Glad shouts have been replaced by dragging feet. He's jaded and stale compared to the vigor and joy that once marked his life and ministry.

Let's be gracious to this Son of Korah, who vulnerably laments the condition of his soul. Think of the risk and possible consequences of this kind of public confession. Remember, he's not a worship leader journaling privately about his doubts in a coffee shop — this psalm was written for public consumption in congregational worship. It was published in Israel's hymnbook for everyone to see and sing.

In the psalm, he admits losing passion for his job. He arrives late to work. He's unsure of his faith in God anymore. As someone charged with connecting others to God, now he's the one who has lost connection. As a lead pastor, I'm not sure how pleased I would be if one of my staff members confessed this to the church. I wonder if King David was pleased with this humble confession or did this Son of Korah lose his job?

God is telling us something about the nature of public confession here. It involves the full disclosure of our sin, doubt, and weakness. Confession exposes us to potential rejection. But it also brings relief once we take the risk, as we walk out of the darkness and into the light. The Apostle John reminds us that, when we publicly confess, we experience forgiveness from God and fellowship with one another: "But if we walk in the light, as he is in the light, we have fellowship with one another, and the blood of Jesus, his Son, purifies us from all sin" (1 Jn 1:7). In Psalm 32, David pulls no punches when he describes the consequences of hiding sin, and the relief of bringing them into the light:

> *For when I kept silent my bones*
>   *wasted away through my groaning all day long,*
> *For day and night your hand was heavy upon me,*
> *My strength was dried up as by the heat of summer.*
> *I acknowledged my sin, I did not cover my iniquity,*
> *I said, 'I will confess my transgressions to the Lord,*
> *And you forgave the iniquity of my sin…*
> *Shout for joy all you upright in heart.*

Psalm 32:3-5, 11

According to David, lack of confession corroded his physical and emotional health, whereas confession produced joy.

In the coming chapter I want to help you to discern between sin, wounds and weakness when it comes to the diagnosis of a saturated soul. Certainly, not all of our soul saturation comes from our sin. That said, it is vital to acknowledge we are sinful.

One of my favorite Americanisms is the simple, yet powerfully humble saying, 'My bad.' I first heard it in the context of softball, which is a sport I learned to play when I first arrived stateside. If someone dropped a catch or struck out they would say 'my bad' to their teammates. Eventually I came to understand what this meant: "The mistake was my fault. I'm not blaming anyone else. I'm taking ownership and I'm sorry." The team's response was generally, "You're good!" I came to realize that this did not mean the person was actually good at softball — it meant they were forgiven for being bad at softball!

The more I heard this exchange, the more it struck me as a picture of the gospel. With God we often try to blame-shift to justify ourselves, as if to say, "I'm good." But it's only when we say "my bad," confessing our guilt that we hear God say, "You're good. I forgive you and declare you righteous by grace." This beautiful reality is proclaimed in Psalm 103:11-12: "As high as the heavens are above the earth, so great is his steadfast to those who fear Him. As far as the West is from the East, so far has he taken our sins from us."

FORGIVENESS

While forgiveness towards others is not explicit in Psalm 42, it is implied. One of the causes of the Psalmist's saturated soul is that enemies are mocking his faith: "My tears have been my food day and night, while they say to me all the day long, "'Where is your God?'"

Then again, in verses 9-10, he's taunted:

Why do I go mourning because of the oppression of the enemy?
As with a deadly wound in my bones, my adversaries taunt me,
while they say to me all the day long, "Where is your God?"
Psalm 42:9-10

This isn't good natured teasing from skeptical friends; it's brutal mocking that kicks him while he's down. For the Psalmist, the pain has transcended lighthearted attempts to "be a good sport" or have a thicker skin. We all know that nursery rhymes about sticks and stones fall flat in the real world. According to the psalmist, words can inflict mortal wounds.

In his injured state the author turns to God and pours out his soul, remembering God as his hope and salvation.

He stands his ground with his hope in God. Marianne Williamson once said that unforgiveness is like drinking poison and waiting for the person who hurt you to die.[14] It's a ludicrous idea, but it drives home the point. We often refuse to forgive those who have hurt us, naively hoping they'll get hurt; but actually, we're just hurting ourselves. Unforgiveness is an act of self-harm. The psalmist avoids this trap by committing his wounds to the care of the Great Physician.

In his book, *Reflection on the Psalms*, C.S. Lewis writes extensively on the theme of forgiveness, specifically as seen in the imprecatory psalms (psalms in which the author prays for his enemies to be punished). Lewis explains that these Psalms reveal wickedness is real in this world, and that the proper human response is indignation and a desire for God's judgment. However, he insists that Christians, who have received mercy instead of justice, must likewise extend mercy when they are mistreated. This cycle of offense and forgiveness, Lewis says, is an ongoing cycle:

---

[14] Marianne Williamson, "Forgiveness: Why Holding onto that Grudge Will Only Hurt You," *Christianity Today Online,* March 31, 2016, https://www.christiantoday.com/article/forgiveness.why.holding.ont o.that.grudge.will.only.hurt.you/83008.htm.

For we find that the work of forgiveness has to be done over and over again. We forgive, we mortify our resentment, a week later some chain of thought carries us back to the original offense and we discover the old resentment blazing away as if nothing has been done at all. We need to forgive our brother seventy times seven not only for 490 offenses, but for one offense.[15]

Corrie Ten Boom, a Jewish prisoner of war in Nazi Germany, speaks of finding grace to forgive guards who tortured her and murdered so many of her people. In her struggle to forgive, she was helped by a Lutheran pastor:[16]

Up in that church tower," he said, nodding out the window, "is a bell which is rung by pulling on a rope. But you know what? After the sexton lets go of the rope, the bell keeps on swinging. First ding then dong. Slower and slower until there's a final dong and it stops. I believe the same thing is true of forgiveness. When we forgive someone, we take our hand off the rope. But if we've been tugging at our grievances for a long time, we mustn't be surprised if the old angry thoughts keep coming for a while. They're just the ding-dongs of the old bell slowing down.

In Psalm 42, it's like the author takes his hand off the rope of bitterness, until his enemies' taunting grows ever-

---

[15] C.S. Lewis, *Reflections on the Psalms* (United Kingdom: Harcourt, Brace, 1958) 25.

[16] Ken Baker, *Our Father: Living the Lord's Prayer* (N.p.: Lulu.com, 2017) 91.

fainter in his ears. This is the reward of a soul poured repeatedly out in forgiveness. If we give it time, grace will hold sway and forgiveness will do its slow, steady work.

THREE DANGERS OF AN OVERSATURATED SOUL

What happens if we fail to pour out our souls to God? I think the dangers are at least three-fold.

Danger #1: Getting stuck in the past

Remembering what God has done is important, as the psalmist does, but remembrance can easily get caught in the rip tide of nostalgia. It's tempting to wallow in the present because of the glories of the past. When we start living in the past, dissatisfaction ensues. The band U2 warns of this debilitating nostalgia in their song, "God Part II":[17]

> *Don't believe in the 60's*
> *The golden age of pop*
> *You glorify the past*
> *When the future dries up*

When nostalgia takes root we lose a sense of the future because we romanticize the past. Our emotional muscles at-

---

[17] U2, "God Part II," Genius, 1998, accessed March 10, 2002, https://genius.com/U2-god-part-ii-lyrics.

rophy. Don't let past blessings stunt your emotional health; look back with a grateful heart--then move on with an expectant heart.

Danger #2: Faking it

There is a tremendous temptation to act like we have it all together and to deny it when we don't. Kathy Keller warns about the lure of feigning spiritual health, especially for those in Christian leadership:

> *I've come to believe very strongly that the pull to becoming a worse Christian—cold, distant from God, hypocritical, and even involved in burn-down-your-life scandals—is far stronger when you're ministering to others than are the benefits that may accrue by daily association with spiritual things.*
>
> *One explanation that's almost always suggested is that the Devil takes a greater interest in attacking those who speak for Christ (and I'm including both lay men and women as well as those in "professional ministry") so as to derail their influence for the gospel. However, what's done to us by the forces of darkness is nothing compared to what we do to ourselves.*
>
> *The day will come when you have to deliver a sermon, or counsel someone in need, or listen to a heartsick soul, and you will be in no fit condition to do it. Your prayer life may be lagging, or you have an unreconciled relationship that needs attention, or any number of things may have interrupted your communion with God and your rejoicing in the gospel. When that day arrives, you must sit down, at whatever expense of time and ruination*

to your schedule, and get right with God. Then, and only then,
should you attempt to minister in his name.

Hypocrisy is alarmingly easy to justify. Honesty means we may suffer or damage our reputations, which seems too painful. We convince ourselves that coming clean will wreck the faith of those who depend on us. But in reality, the pain of humbly confessing the state of our souls is far less than the casualties that come from excusing hypocrisy. Confession is the way we escape the clutches of hypocrisy and learn to befriend integrity.

Danger #3: Exploding

The third and final danger shows that, if we refuse to pour out our souls to God, our souls will burst forth on their own in unhealthy ways. We will explode. Unhealthy people have tiny triggers and huge reactions. We bottle up toxins in our soul for so long that they eventually burst out, causing real damage to ourselves and others. An example of this comes in Numbers 20, when Moses strikes the rock instead of speaking to it.

The Israelites had been grumbling, per their usual pattern. Moses had just lost his sister, Miriam. Thus, in the midst of his grief, their grumbling triggers an explosion in

Moses. Instead of speaking to the rock, he strikes the rock in a burst of frustration.

Surprisingly, God still graciously causes water to gush from the rock. It appears Moses is on track. Yet his rash actions disqualify him from entering the land of promise. In striking the rock, he ultimately strikes out. This is a sobering warning to all of us: exploding has consequences.

So, how do we avoid these three dangers — getting stuck in the past, faking it, and exploding?

I'm afraid there are no quick-fixes. No silver bullets. There's no getting around the grunt work of soul health. But there are many helpful practices, means of grace that aid us in pouring out our souls: journaling, letter writing, hiking, running, swimming, fishing, songwriting, painting, reading poetry, or processing with an empathetic friend or counselor. I've found a combination of verbal, physical and written practices to be most helpful. One of the most memorable practices was taking a few days to walk through the Stations of the Cross while staying at a monastery near the ocean. Knowing it would be intense I took my paddle board and interspersed walking the stations with paddle surfing and journaling. I had a guide book from my spiritual director that helped me to pray meaningfully at each station.

I remember being most deeply impacted at the station of Christ's betrayal by Judas. I had felt betrayed by three people that year. I was able to bring my painful experience of betrayal to Jesus, knowing that he was able to sympathize with me. I experienced a release of resentment through forgiveness and took a significant step towards healing.

While this kind of soul work is painful, it is far less painful than the consequences of getting stuck in the past, being called out for faking it, or exploding in anger. As we pour out our souls, we make space for God to pour His living water into our souls by His Spirit.

Isaiah prophesied that a suffering servant would "pour out his soul to death, making intercession for the transgressors" (Is 53:12). Consider how Jesus poured out his soul to death for you on the cross. Christ poured out his soul to death, so that now when we pour out our souls to him, we receive life.

CHAPTER 4:
LISTEN TO YOUR SOUL

Why are you cast down, O my soul, and why are you in turmoil within me?

Psalm 42:5

"My soul is dispersed," said Lucas as he wept on our couch.

"Can you try and explain that for us?" my wife and I asked, empathetic but confused.

When Lucas described his soul as "dispersed," he was thinking of the Portuguese word *disperso* to express what he was feeling. *Disperso* means "scattered," and based on his story, it's no wonder. Lucas is an immigrant, just like my family when we arrived in the U.S. He came from Brazil on a soccer scholarship, but his student visa doesn't permit him to earn extra money. After meeting an American girl and wanting to get married, Lucas has no way to provide. Beyond driving Uber and working odd jobs for cash, there is really nothing he can do if he wants to gain permanent residency. As we listened to his words that day, in a real sense we were helping him listen to his own soul.

Articulating the condition of our souls is hard work. It takes some brave inquiry and, for many, a new vocabulary. Particularly with men, whose emotional fluency is often limited, it's a struggle to articulate feelings beyond general descriptors like "angry" or "stressed out."

Pete Scazzero, an expert on emotional health writes, "Emotional health and spiritual maturity are inseparable."[18] It is not possible "to be spiritually mature while remaining emotionally immature."[19] That's why, in my own life, I've seen a spiritual director every month for the past five years. It's helpful to be asked questions that draw out what I'm feeling. Counseling has helped me listen to my soul. I also encourage emotional health for my team — once I gave each pastor on the team a bookmark with about 50 emotions to

---

[18] Peter Scazzero, *Emotionally Healthy Spirituality: It's Impossible to Be Spiritually Mature, While Remaining Emotionally Immature* (United States: Zondervan, 2017), 12.

[19] Ibid., title.

choose from, to help them improve their emotional vocabulary. The aim of listening to our souls is not to become fixated with our emotional world; it's to find out what blocks us from connecting with God and people. The connection between emotional health and spiritual maturity is crucial, yet so often ignored.

In Psalm 42, God invites us to become emotionally healthy so that we can become spiritually healthy. Notice how the psalmist talks to himself: "Why, oh my soul are you so cast down within me?" The description of his soul as "downcast" is significant: The Hebrew word used here is *shachach* and it has a bandwidth of meaning. It includes a general feeling of gloominess, but extends all the way to utter despair and emotional collapse. Those who suffer from clinical depression and trauma-induced anxiety can take comfort that their struggles are dignified in this psalm. The author is weighed down by emotional turmoil, as if there's a massive wave pummeling him: "All your waves and breakers have crashed over me" (Ps 42:7b).

If you surf, you know what it's like to get caught inside a set of breakers. You're pinned down until your lungs are bursting. You fight to reach the surface, gasping for breath, just as another wave dumps its weight on you. You often lose a sense of which way is up or down, and the sense of disorientation can be terrifying. When you eventually make it back to shore, the ocean water stings your sinuses as it rushes out.

The complexity of the cultural moment — whether racial tension, politics, masks, COVID gathering protocols, vaccines or Russia's invasion of Ukraine — has left me exhausted and conflicted. People's polarized opinions have given me whiplash. These are people I love. Many are close friends. Some are on the team I lead. They all love Jesus, yet still have conflicting convictions. And they seem so certain of themselves. I never thought I'd say it, but I find myself longing for a little more uncertainty. Instead of humble conviction, which leaves room to be partially wrong, people vehemently try to persuade me to see things their way. Sometimes I agree with them but simply do not feel as strongly as they do. Other times I think they're crazy! What if they leave the church when I disagree with them? I feel decision fatigue, conflict fatigue, debate fatigue. Can you relate?

THE THING BEHIND THE THING

It's not enough for the psalmist to know the condition of his soul — he wants to know why, so he interrogates his soul: "Why, Oh my soul, are you in turmoil?" (Ps. 42:5). He follows up with another question, "Why so cast down within me?" (Ps. 42:5). He is not satisfied with the symptom (depression and turmoil); he wants to understand the root cause. He's searching for what I call the "thing behind the thing." This isn't an exact science. It requires a willingness to sit with our emotions, listen, articulate what we hear and sense, and invite others to help us make sense of it all.

We often associate spiritual courage with a kind of stiff upper lip stoicism, but instead of repressing emotions, Psalm 42 encourages us to examine them. If we do not understand the thing behind the thing, we will come up with faulty solutions. Taylor Swift's lyric comes to mind: "Band-Aids don't fix bullet holes."[20] Sometimes we need to simply ask ourselves: Why, oh, my soul? As it turns out, courage often looks like curiosity.

Again, Pete Scazzero offers wisdom:

When we deny our pain, losses, and feelings year after year, we become less and less human. We transform slowly into empty shells with smiley faces painted on them...But when I began to allow myself to feel a wider range of emotions, including sadness, depression, fear, and anger, a revolution in my spirituality was

---

[20] Taylor Swift, "Bad Blood," Genius, 2014, accessed March 11, 2002, https://genius.com/Taylor-swift-bad-blood-lyrics.

unleashed. I soon realized that a failure to appreciate the biblical place of feelings within our larger Christian lives has done extensive damage, keeping free people in Christ in slavery.[21]

So, while it's destructive to glorify feelings, to ignore them is to stifle God's work in our lives. But paying attention to our emotions is complex and difficult, thus we need some categories for understanding them.

WOUNDS, WEAKNESS, AND WAR

D.A. Carson reflects on David's complex emotions in Psalm 38, "At best David is transparently honest. When there is an array of things going wrong in his life he does not collapse them into one single problem."[22]

We should beware of the simplistic diagnosis that all our problems are the consequences of personal sin, and that the remedy is *always* repentance. As the saying goes: "If all you have is a hammer, everything looks like a nail." Sometimes a hammer isn't the right tool, and when we swing away at a

---

[21] Scazzero, *Emotionally Healthy Spirituality*, 70.

[22] D. A. Carson, *For the Love of God* (Vol. 1, Trade Paperback): *A Daily Companion for Discovering the Riches of God's Word* (United States: Crossway, 2006), 27.

fragile soul, it shatters what should be mended. Beyond sin and repentance (which are important), scripture provides other categories for understanding the turmoil in our souls: wounds, weakness, and war.

Wounds

One of the categories we find in Psalm 42 is wounds, as seen in verse 10: "As with a deadly wound in my bones, my enemies taunt me." Regardless of whether the author is guilty of personal sin, it's clear he's been sinned *against*. The sins of others have slashed him, and he's bleeding out.

Darrin Patrick, an American pastor who tragically took his own life in 2019, drew this helpful distinction between sin and wounds:[23]

> *We often get sin and wounds confused. Sins are rebellious places in our hearts that need repenting. Wounds are tender places in our hearts that need healing. You cannot repent of wounds and you cannot go to therapy for sins.*

---

[23] Tony Jones, "Darrin Patrick: 'There's Something about the Woods,'" The Reverend Hunter Podcast, May 18, 2020, https://podcasts.apple.com/us/podcast/darrin-patrick-theres-something-about-the-woods/id1500247799?i=1000474969379.

Yet, while sins and wounds are distinct, they're also related, as Darrin's wife once shared with me directly: "Darrin and I often used to say that unhealed wounds often become fertile soil in which sin grows. Of course, both need to be taken to our merciful God."

The importance of understanding how sin and wounds relate, and how they differ, can't be underestimated. When someone sins against you, you're left with a wound that must be tended to. Without treatment, wounds fester, eventually turning septic. The more toxic you become, the more likely it is that you'll sin against others. While you should repent for that sin, it still won't cure you of *the thing behind the thing*, which is the wound. The healing of this wound requires extending mercy in order to receive mercy, sending the person who has wounded me away debt free in order to experience freedom myself. The healing of a soul wound is more gradual than a moment of repentance. But as it heals, turmoil is gradually replaced by clarity and peace.

The metaphor I would use to distinguish them is the treatment of a tumor versus that of a burn wound. Sin is like a tumor that must be cut out rapidly with the scalpel of repentance. A burn wound cannot be cut out. It must be slowly nursed back to health through application of a salve. Similarly, soul wounds are healed gradually via the salve of forgiveness, empathetic counseling, healing prayer, and the work of the Holy Spirit.

Weakness

Another scriptural category that causes turmoil in our souls is weakness. This is distinct from wounds in that it may not be the result of what someone did to me, but rather what my parents gave to me. Weakness refers to an inherited genetic frailty such as alcoholism, anxiety, depression, dyslexia or cerebral palsy. One way or another, we all walk with a limp. While this is a result of original sin, it cannot be repented of and cannot be healed in the same way that a wound can. It is what the Apostle Paul refers to as his "thorn in the flesh," some unknown ailment that, despite his prayers, God doesn't remove. Instead, God says, "My grace is sufficient for you because my power is made perfect in weakness" (2 Cor 12:9).

My aunt Patricia (I call her "Pat") was born with cerebral palsy. She is a Christian and has been prayed for many times to be healed, but has remained physically disabled. While her mind and spirit are sharp, she cannot walk, eat, talk without slurring her speech, or bathe herself. This weakness has taken a toll on Pat's soul over the years. Despite graduating from college, running a business, and even learning to ride a horse, she's often discouraged to be so dependent on others. She frequently feels excluded and struggles with a sense of rejection. She gets frustrated when people struggle to understand her speech. She is stiff and bent over from decades of sitting in a wheelchair, which can wear on her emotions just as much as her body. The toll that this weakness has taken on Pat's soul is not the result of sin to be repented of, or even a wound from someone else's sin that can be healed through forgiveness (although she has had to do both). This kind of long-term weakness requires a long-term grace that only God can give.

War

The third category is what I call war. This category recognizes that Satan is the enemy of our souls who preys on our sin, wounds and weakness to keep our souls submerged in turmoil. He's like a bully in the ocean who pushes our heads under the waves and holds us there, suffocating us with condemnation, fear, and bitterness. Spiritual warfare is a complex topic. But it seems to relate, in part, to the emotional state of our souls. The Apostle Paul describes his thorn in the flesh as a "messenger from Satan" (2 Cor 12:7). Apparently, he understood that his weakness had a spiritual warfare component to it.

The most dramatic example of the correlation between the state of a person's soul and the demonic realm is the account of the demon possessed man from the Gerasenes. His description is intimidating: he was impossible to subdue, even with chains, because of his demonic, supernatural strength. Luke's gospel summarizes the state of his soul as follows: "Night and day among the tombs and on the mountains he was always crying out and cutting himself with stones" (Lk 5:5). When Jesus encountered this man, he didn't teach him or try to counsel him, as he did on many other occasions with other people in distress; instead he cast a legion of demons out of him.

Tom and Katy Sappington, American missionaries to Indonesia for 25 years, have written extensively on this topic. Having returned to America they spend their time helping people with a materialist view of soul care develop a category for spiritual warfare. They use the idea of rats and trash to explain the connection. In his book, Letting God be the Judge, Tom explains that demons are like rats that roam around in the dark seeking to infest people's lives. Emotional wounds that are untended to are like a person who leaves trash lying around their house at night. The trash of unforgiveness, bitterness and ungodly judgements against people who have sinned against us, attract the rats which then come and infest the house of our lives. They explain that it is no use trying to chase the rats away unless we are willing to throw away the trash. Once the trash has been removed, it is easier to dispel the rats.

They use the techniques they call "visualizing prayer" and "authoritative prayer," helping people to take out the trash that plagues their memories. This leads to more authoritative prayer that aims to dispel the presence of demonic strongholds in people's lives. Both my wife and I have spent many hours with Tom and Katy and have experienced significant freedom from our time with them. Their ministry is understated and undramatic, yet undeniably dynamic.

THE WAY FORWARD

So how do you discern whether a particular struggle is caused by sin, wounds, weakness, and war — or a combination of several?

There are many helpful tools that will help you understand your wiring. Personally I've benefited from personality tests like the Myers-Briggs, StrengthsFinder, and Enneagram.

Each one uses a unique framework that, if used wisely, can help you listen to your soul. As followers of Christ, we should be wary of slavish loyalty to any man-made framework for understanding ourselves. While they can be useful, eventually every trend will be displaced and forgotten. Ultimately, the Bible's wisdom about the soul is timeless — when the Enneagram is a faded footnote in the annals of history, scripture will remain relevant.

We also need other people to help understand ourselves, whether friends, a spouse, counselor, family, or the body of Christ. Ask someone close to you: How do you experience me when I'm upset? How do I act differently when I am emotionally healthy vs. unhealthy? This kind of feedback, while sometimes hard to hear, is vital because it reveals blind spots. Outside perspective is a gift, not a curse, so invite trusted voices to reflect your own soul back to you.

So use tools, lean on others, but ultimately — look to Christ. He not only understands these categories plaguing our souls (wounds, weakness, war), but he offers the remedy for each.

Christ was wounded.

It is a beautiful comfort to remember that Jesus chose to be clothed in weakness in his humanity. One of the most emphatic expressions of his weakness was that he was willing to be wounded by those he created, those who he came to save. Edward Shillito wrote a short poem in 1919 that described Jesus as a unique Savior who embraced both wounds and weakness. It is called "Jesus of the Scars"[24]:

> *The other gods were strong; but Thou wast weak;*
> *They rode, but Thou didst stumble to a throne;*
> *But to our wounds only God's wounds can speak,*
> *And not a god has wounds, but Thou alone.*

Christ became weak.

Though he was fully God, he lived with human limitations on his energy, knowledge and emotions. As a child he had to depend on a mother and father for sustenance and protection. He had to flee as a refugee with his family from a violent king. As a boy he had to learn a language. Learn a trade. Grow in strength. As a man he got drained. He felt frustrated. He experienced grief, loneliness and temptation. Jesus had to withdraw often to recharge. Hebrews tells us

---

[24] Mark Dever, *The Message of the New Testament: Promises Kept* (United States: Crossway Books, 2005) 119.

that he was "beset by weakness" in order to sympathize with us in our weakness (Heb 5:2).

Christ is victorious.

It is marvelous that our Savior, who embraced weakness and experienced woundedness, crushed the head of the serpent in his death (Gen 3:15). What looked like weakness and defeat on the cross was actually victory. Jesus disarmed demonic powers and authorities making a public spectacle of them, triumphing over them by the cross (Col 2:15). This hidden triumph burst into view through his resurrection.

The call to listen to our souls is not a self-help remedy. It's an invitation to commune with Jesus, who understands our wounds because he was wounded, empathizes with our weakness because he became weak, and who wins our battles as the victorious King.

CHAPTER 5:

SPEAK TO YOUR SOUL

Oh, my soul, Put your hope in God. Why so cast down Oh my soul? Hope in God; for I shall again praise him, my salvation and my God."

Psalm 42:11

They say talking to yourself is the first sign of madness. I beg to differ.

Naturally, mumbling to oneself CAN be a sign of mental illness, and I don't mean to diminish that, but self-talk can also be a sign of emotional health. Listening to your soul is one thing — having the courage to speak to your soul is altogether different. For me, it's been the difference between sinking into a pit of despair and moving toward true hope. Self-talk is an underrated power in our 'keep it real' culture.

I'm all for authenticity. I've already mentioned the dangers of faking it and the permission the psalms give to be brutally honest with ourselves, God, and others. But when authenticity becomes an idol, we get perpetually stuck in our brokenness, unable to move toward wholeness.

Benjamin Franklin wrote: "A man wrapped up in himself is a very small bundle."[25] What does it mean to be honest with ourselves without getting wrapped up in ourselves? How do we build our emotions upon truth rather than the ever-changing mood of the moment?

Psalm 42 offers guidance. In verse 5, the psalmist has a dialogue with his own soul: "Why, oh my soul, are you cast down within me and why in turmoil? Put your hope in God, for he is my salvation and my God."

The psalmist repeats this same pattern of self-inquiry and self-talk in verse 11: "Why so cast down, O my soul? Hope in God; for I shall again praise him, my salvation and my God."

While ignoring our souls is dangerous, there's an equally perilous habit of listening to ourselves for too long. Having

---

[25] Benjamin Franklin and Amy Gutmann, *The Autobiography of Benjamin Franklin* (Penn Reading Project Edition; Ukraine: University of Pennsylvania Press, Incorporated, 2010), xi.

listened, you and I need to speak truth to our souls through Scripture-saturated, Spirit-led self-talk. Paul Tripp, the author of *How the Gospel Changes Us,* writes: "No one is more influential in your life than you are because no one talks to you more than you do."[26] Whether audibly or silently, we talk to ourselves all the time. Our souls chatter away incessantly, thus we need a way to shift our monologues into dialogues. Self-talk is not screaming "Shut up!" to our souls — it's engaging our souls with God's truth. It's leading our souls to put their hope in God.

No one has provided me with more insight into emotional health in the Psalms than Dr. Martin Lloyd Jones. In 1965, many years before soul care was an acknowledged topic among evangelical Christians, Lloyd-Jones wrote an extensive work on the Psalms called Spiritual Depression: Its Causes and Its Cure. In the book, he poses this potent question about the power of self-talk: "Have you realized that most of your unhappiness in life is due to the fact that you are listening to yourself instead of talking to yourself?"[27]

---

[26] Paul Tripp, *New Morning Mercies: A Daily Gospel Devotional* (United States: Crossway, 2014), 4.

[27] D. Martyn Lloyd-Jones, *Spiritual Depression: Its Causes and Cure,* (United States: Eerdmans Publishing Company, 1965), 20.

Let's pause there for a moment. Do you believe this? Is it really necessary to talk to yourself, not just listen to yourself? If Lloyd-Jones is right, this challenges the spirit of our age, which enslaves us by demanding we obey every whim of our souls. Could it be that this psalm gives us a healthy way to answer our souls — even *debate* with our souls? Lloyd-Jones gives an example of what this internal discourse might look like:

Take those thoughts that come to you the moment you wake up in the morning. You have not originated them, but there they are, talking to you. They bring back the problem of yesterday. Somebody's talking. Who's talking? Your self is talking to you. Now this man's treatment in Psalm 42 was this: instead of allowing his self to talk to him, he starts talking to himself, "Why are you cast down, O my soul?" he asks. His soul had been depressing him, crushing him. So he stands up and says: "Self, listen for a moment, I will speak to you."[28]

In Psalm 42:5, the author speaks commandingly to himself: "My soul, put your hope in God." While he acknowledges his internal turmoil, he refuses to indulge it. He knows that his soul's only hope comes from God. The Hebrew word 'hope' here is *yachal*, which means to wait expectantly.

---

[28] Ibid., 20-21.

Despite feeling trapped under the relentless breakers of depression this Son of Korah is directing his soul to wait expectantly for God to save him from his sea of sorrow.

WORSHIP

Beyond hope, the psalmist counsels his soul to *worship* God: "Put your hope in God, for I shall again praise Him." This seems outrageous. How can someone praise God while being crushed by breakers of depression? Isn't this the epitome of faking it? Dodging lament, or suppressing emotion, is unhealthy, yet scripture consistently prods us to worship in the midst of disorientation, as seen in Psalm 103:1-5:

Bless the Lord, O my soul,
and all that is within me,
bless his holy name!
Bless the Lord, O my soul,
and forget not all his benefits,
who forgives all your iniquity,
who heals all your diseases,
who redeems your life from the pit,
who crowns you with steadfast love and mercy,
who satisfies you with good
so that your youth is renewed like the eagle's.

In this psalm, David instructs his own soul, much like a parent would instruct their child to be attentive and gracious to dinner guests. He rehearses all the blessings God has provided, arming himself with reasons to wholeheartedly praise God. Tim Keller, speaking on this portion of Psalm 103, says: "He's addressing himself. And that's not prayer, but that's also not just reading the Bible. That is learning how to take what he's read in the Bible and screw it down into his heart until it catches on fire."[29]

We praise God because he is worth it. I wish I always lived this way, but honestly it's not always enough to motivate me. Yes, it's right to give God glory, but giving him glory is also good for me. Worship is what my soul needs most of all. This remembrance has served me well in times of turmoil and sorrow.

In his marvelous book, *Reflection on the Psalms*, C.S. Lewis explains the connection between praising God and enjoying God:

Praise almost seems to be inner health made audible. I think we delight to praise what we enjoy because the praise not merely expresses but completes the enjoyment, it is its appointed

---

[29] Tish Harrison Warren, "How a Cancer Diagnosis Makes Jesus' Death and Resurrection Mean More," *New York Times,* April 10, 2022, https://www.nytimes.com/2022/04/10/opinion/timothy-keller-cancer-easter.html.

consummation. It is not out of compliment that lovers keep on telling one another how beautiful they are; the delight is incomplete until it is expressed. The Scottish catechism tells us that the chief end of man is to glorify God and enjoy him forever. But one day we shall know that the two are one and the same thing. Fully to enjoy is to glorify.[30]

Our enjoyment of God is incomplete until it is expressed. Our hope in God is muted until it is uttered. This is why worship makes sense in seemingly desperate times: it reminds us that sorrow isn't our ultimate destination, nor are circumstances our ultimate hope.

Lewis continues this theme in his well-known allegory on spiritual warfare, *The Screwtape Letters.* In the book, a senior devil (Screwtape) writes coaching letters to his nephew devil (Wormwood), coaching him on how to ruin the faith of a recent Christian convert:

The best thing, where it is possible, is to keep the patient from the serious intention of praying altogether......At the very least, they can be persuaded that the bodily position makes no difference to their prayers; for they constantly forget, what you must always remember, that they are animals and that whatever their bodies do affects their souls. It is funny how mortals

---

[30] Lewis, *Reflections on the Psalms*, 94.

always picture us as putting things into their minds: in reality our best work is done by keeping things out.[31]

Satan would love to convince us that what we do with our bodies has no effect on our souls. But God has created the body and soul to be connected, therefore, when I kneel to pray or raise my hands in worship, the posture of my body affects my soul. I've found that kneeling in worship and prayer helps a great deal if I am wrestling between God's will and my own. The posture of my body affects the posture of my soul. If I'm feeling downcast, I don't suppress that feeling, but I find that lifting my hands in worship is far better for me than folding my arms or thrusting them deep into my pockets. What we do externally impacts who we are internally.

Our culture preaches the gospel of self, which means obeying our desires, feelings, and impulses. But the Christian gospel calls us to acknowledge the good and bad of our emotions, and to invite Jesus to transform our broken areas. Sometimes it's good to listen to your soul; it's often better to speak to your soul.

---

[31] C. S. Lewis, *The Screwtape Letters* (South Korea: HarperCollins, 2001) 15.

When our children were young and their feelings were getting the better of them, my wife would have them repeat this phrase: "I am the boss of my feelings." As they grew older, we adapted the phrase to: "Feelings are a wonderful servant but a terrible master!" Sometimes parents, not wanting to stifle their kids' emotions, allow their children to be mastered by them. But emotional unruliness is just as dangerous as emotional repression. Fred Rogers, the beloved children's television host, says it well: "Anything that's human is mentionable, and anything that is mentionable can be more manageable. When we can talk about our feelings, they become less overwhelming, less upsetting, and less scary. The people we trust with that important talk can help us know that we are not alone."[32] I love this. Emotions are both mentionable and manageable.

If this is true then emotional health means honoring biblical truth above my own fickle sense of reality. I do not ignore my soul. But in the light of sin's corruption, I don't take

---

[32] Deborah Farmer Kris, "What's Mentionable is Manageable: Why Parents Should Help Children Name their Fears," *The Washington Post online,* Sept. 20, 2018, https://www.washingtonpost.com/news/ Parenting/wp/2018/09/20/whats-mentionable-is-manageable-why-parents-should-help-kids-name-their-fears.

my soul too seriously. In doing so, I fly in the face of our culture's mantra which is, "Be true to yourself." The Psalms point us in a healthier direction: "Be honest with yourself. Be true to God."

Most Fridays I surf at Doheny Beach in South Orange County. There is a rocky jetty that juts out into the surf with an anvil shaped rock at its point. It's known as "the hammer." The Doheny rule is that paddle boarders have to surf south of the hammer. Because of the shifting tides, as well as my own absent-mindedness, I sometimes look up and realize I've drifted too far north to be legal, or too far south to catch a wave. The hammer provides a helpful point of reference amidst the inevitable ocean drift.

Similarly, our emotions are like ever-shifting currents. They're not all negative, but unpredictable and unreliable. We need an external, immovable point to anchor our souls in turbulent waters.

INDESTRUCTIBLE HAPPINESS

As we interrupt our soul's chatter with the unchanging truth of God's Word, what might be a helpful way to do so? I've found Jonathan Edwards' essay on Christian Happiness to be a helpful framework. In his essay, he distills the secret of Christian happiness down to three truths from the Apostle Paul's famous discourse in Romans 8.[33]

All our good things cannot be taken away.
All our bad things will come to pass.
All our best things are yet to come.

If we look at Edwards' statements through the lens of Romans 8 we can understand they are solid statements, not empty cliches. The Apostle Paul writes that our adoption as God's dear children cannot be taken away; that absolutely nothing can separate us from the love of our Father in Christ Jesus. All our good things cannot be taken away.

He insists that God is working in all things—even the worst things—for His glory and our good if we are his. Even our weakness is working for our good as the Spirit groans in intercession for us. All our bad things will come to pass.

He argues that our momentary sufferings cannot compare to the weight of glory that awaits us. In fact, he writes, all of creation groans in anticipation of the glory that will be

---

[33] Quoted in Timothy Keller, *Prayer: Experiencing Awe and Intimacy with God* (United States: Penguin Publishing Group, 2014), 232.

revealed to us and through us. Our groaning will turn to rejoicing on that day. All our best things are yet to come.

On my bad days, I speak these gospel truths to my soul. I am not silencing my soul so much as answering its melancholic, nervous chatter with anchoring truth. My soul so easily drifts from faith and wisdom, carried off by the treacherous tides of deception and fear. Thank God for Jesus, whose unchanging grace and word are an anchor for my soul.

When darkness veils His lovely face
I rest on His unchanging grace
In every high and stormy gale
My anchor holds within the veil

CHAPTER 6:
RECONNECT YOUR SOUL

These things I remember as I pour out my soul: how I would go with the throng and lead them in procession to the house of God with glad shouts and songs of praise, a multitude keeping festival.

Psalm 42:4

Matt was on summer break in Cancún, Mexico. Adriana worked as a manager at his resort. Both young and single, they hit it off, especially when Matt won the Ironman competition at the hotel swimming pool.

Their summer romance quickly turned into a marriage proposal: Matt asked Adriana to marry him and move to the United States. Within two years of meeting, they started their new life together in California. But a few years in, marital bliss rapidly faded as Adriana wrestled to adjust to a new land, language, and culture. Homesickness and loneliness set in. Matt, feeling powerless to help his new bride, poured his energy into his growing business. If he couldn't heal her pain perhaps he could ease it by providing a comfortable life for her.

But when financial provision didn't solve their growing tension, Matt nursed a growing resentment and the emotional chasm between them widened. That's when Adriana got pregnant, and after giving birth to their first daughter, the fighting escalated. When they fought, Adriana threatened to take their daughter back to Mexico. In response, Matt began researching legal ways to maintain custody in the case of divorce.

Like a Hail Mary pass in the final seconds of a football game, they decided to attend our church on Easter Sunday. Although they had different religious upbringings (Matt grew up Christian but had wandered from the faith, while Adriana grew up Catholic), they nonetheless hoped church might provide Adriana with friends to quell her homesickness. Perhaps someone there could counsel their crumbling marriage back toward health. Their prayers were answered: they began meeting with Kevin and Shannon, a couple on our pastoral team who had worked through their own broken marriage after becoming Christians.

In this new environment of support, Matt and Adriana's relationship steadily began to heal. Instead of trying to fix her, Matt repented of his selfishness and anger, and recommitted his life to Christ. Adriana opened up about childhood abuse and the trauma it unleashed in her life. God began to heal her wounds. A year after arriving at Southlands, Adriana was baptized as a follower of Christ. Matt met regularly with a group of men who taught him how to be a servant leader in his marriage.

Today, they are almost unrecognizable from the couple that limped into our Easter service eight years ago. They are a vital part of our pastoral team, helping many other marriages grow to a place of health and strength. Looking back on that first Sunday, Adriana says: "I was hoping to find a friend, but what I found is a family."

CREATED FOR COMMUNITY

I think we underestimate how much God's presence is expressed to us through other Christians. This is why, in Psalm 42, the author laments his distance from God's people. In verse 6 he writes: "My soul is cast down within me; therefore I remember you from the land of Jordan and of Hermon, from Mount Mizar." Those locations don't mean much for most of us, but for the psalmist, they indicate he is miles from Jerusalem and the tabernacle. We aren't told why he's in the land of the Jordan, so far from home, but the displacement has depleted his soul.

This psalm reminds us that separation from Christian community is harmful. Today the danger is even greater, as individualism enables us to be physically close to one another, while remaining relationally isolated. Psychiatrist Larry Crabb explains how expressive individualism can negatively impact emotional health:

> *We have made a terrible mistake! For most of this century we have wrongly defined soul wounds as psychological disorders and delegated their treatment to trained specialists. Damaged psyches aren't the problem. The problem is disconnected souls. What we need is connection. What we need is a healing community. Our greatest problem is not damaged psyches. It is disconnected souls.[34]*

Individualism has sold us the lie that committing to others means losing yourself. But as people created in God's image (who is himself relational), we are better together. When God told Adam that it is not good for man to be

---

[34] Quoted in Dave Earley and Ben Gutiérrez, Ben, *Ministry Is . . ..* (United States: B&H Publishing Group, 2010), 285.

alone, he was not merely talking about marriage. He was making a statement about humanity itself. We are hardwired to live *with* others. In the context of community, we learn more about ourselves than if we walk alone.

For instance, I thought I was selfless until I got married to my wife. I thought I was gracious until my friends offended me. I thought I was confident until I encountered pushback from my team. I only discovered who I really was in the context of community. This can be a positive thing — there are times when my own prayers seem to hit the ceiling, but the prayers of others encourage me. When I can't see a solution to a problem, the fresh perspective of others helps me maneuver through the complexity. When others show me grace, it deepens my understanding of God's grace — even my ability to receive it.

FREEDOM IN TENSION

Committing to Christian community can feel more restrictive than total autonomy, but actually it frees our souls to sing, as this parable illustrates:

One day a man entered a music store and watched with fascination as the owner carefully fashioned a violin. Taking four strings out of their package, the owner waved them in front of the observer.

As the strings waved in his hand, he asked: "Do you think these strings are free?"

"Yes, they are free," replied the observer.

The craftsman then anchored the strings to the body of the violin, tightening them until they were taut and in tune. Taking a bow, he played a beautiful melody, looked at the observer and said: "Now these strings are finally free. Free to sing."

This story demonstrates the counterintuitive benefit of community. We tend to think of freedom as the absence of limits or tension in our lives. But actually, it's only when we intentionally embrace the limitations of community that we find true freedom and discover our true purpose. The best way to develop your own voice is to sing with the choir.

Of course, no community is a utopia. Anybody who commits to others will be wounded somehow. Many have experienced deep trauma from various kinds of abuse within faith communities, which sadly drives them into self-protective isolation. Every time a Christian leader leverages power to take advantage of people, it's tempting to abandon the idea of community. I empathize with this skepticism. However, I plead with you to not let disappointment push you into disconnection. You were never meant to follow Christ alone. There are over forty "one another" statements in the New Testament, which demonstrate our interdependence as Christ-followers.

Trauma is real. Healing from it is vital, and those genuinely wounded, abused, or mistreated deserve the utmost care and gentleness. But culturally we tend to overuse terms like "triggered" and "trauma." These legitimate psychological terms have been co-opted to decry the slightest bump or scratch, like a soccer player who feigns an injury so the referee will pull a red card. Not all hurt is trauma. The very nature of community, even healthy community, is that we make ourselves vulnerable and this comes with both joy and pain. C.S. Lewis, provides insight on this in his book, *The Four Loves*:

> *To love at all is to be vulnerable. Love anything and your heart will be wrung and possibly broken. If you want to make sure of keeping it intact you must give it to no one, not even an animal. Wrap it carefully round with hobbies and little luxuries; avoid all entanglements. Lock it up safe in the casket or coffin of your selfishness. But in that casket, safe, dark, motionless, airless, it will change. It will not be broken; it will become unbreakable, impenetrable, irredeemable.[35]*

---

[35] C. S. Lewis, *The Four Loves* (United Kingdom: HarperCollins Publishers, 2010), 159-160.

As Lewis articulates so well, love requires vulnerability. The author of Psalm 42 is very aware of this. He's been wounded by others, perhaps even people he trusted for years. Our natural instinct when we're wounded is to self-protect: to cushion our heart from anything that might break it. But often, the walls we build to keep bad things out also keep good things from getting in. There is always good reason to self-protect but the end of this self-protection is bitterness and isolation.

There's a poisonous plant in Belize called black poisonwood, which causes severe skin damage and pain upon contact:

> *The sap contains alkaloids that cause serious skin and mucus irritations after skin contact. Any part of the tree may carry the sap so handling any part of the poisonwood should be avoided. The cure for the poisonwood tree is the gumbo-limbo tree which is often found growing close to the poisonwood. Bark from the gumbo-limbo should be applied to the affected area, and the wound should be washed three times a day with water in which the bark has been boiled.[36]*

---

[36] "Poisonous Plants of Belize & Central America," *Consejo* Belize, accessed March 28, 2022, http://consejo.bz/belize/poisonplants/poisonplants.html.

I find it fascinating that two plants — one that harms and one that heals — grow side by side. If you've been poisoned by an unhealthy person or community, it's tempting to flee from the forest. But don't allow the toxic trees to keep you from noticing the healing trees two feet away. I say this with tenderness: If you've been wounded by an unhealthy community, you will only heal by reconnecting to a healthy community. This will require bravery as you face potentially triggering situations. But your bravery will be worth it. God is faithful — he will walk beside you every step of the way.

Some people, instead of rejecting Christian community altogether, keep a safe distance by participating digitally, not in-person. On the surface, this seems to offer a way to participate in community with less risk of getting hurt. However, as John Stott pointed out forty years before the online church phenomenon, nothing can replace face-to-face interaction:

> *It is difficult to imagine the world in the year A.D. 2000 by which time versatile micro processers are likely to be as common as simple calculators are today. We should certainly welcome the fact that the silicone chip will transcend human brain power as the machine has transcended human muscle power. Much less welcome will be the probable reduction of human contact as a new electronic network renders personal relationships ever less necessary. In such a dehumanized society the fellowship of the local church will become increasingly important whose members*

meet one another and talk and listen to one another in person rather than on screen. In this human context of mutual love the speaking and hearing of the word of God is also likely to become more necessary for the preservation of our humanness, not less.[37]

As Stott asserts, the embodied church is vital for our humanness. But in our disembodied age, in which people hop from one church to another online, what does it look like to commit wholeheartedly to a local community?

REALISTIC EXPECTATIONS

For a start, we must assess whether our expectations are idealistic or realistic. There's truth in the saying: "If you find the perfect church, don't join it. You'll spoil it." Sometimes we have impossibly high expectations of a church, its leaders and its people — expectations that we would struggle to meet ourselves if they were placed upon us. At the very least, we should have the same standards for a church that we have for ourselves, and extend the same grace towards it that we extend to ourselves. Dietrich Bonhoeffer, in his profound book *Life Together*, gives us a warning in this regard: "The person who loves their dream of community will destroy com-

---

[37] John Stott, *I Believe in Preaching* (United Kingdom: Hoddder and Stouton, 1982), 69.

munity, but the person who loves those around them will create community."[38]

Better to be present with bedhead than absent because you're having a bad hair day. Better to invite someone over once a week for mac and cheese than once a year for prime rib. Even as we long for the ideal, let's resolve to live in the real. We are not in heaven yet.

Scripture never presents God's people as a frictionless bunch. Problems are talked out so that reconciliation can be lived out. Imagine the disciples' anger at Judas' betrayal, or their shame about fleeing in fear during Jesus' arrest. Imagine Peter's shame when he confessed his threefold denial to his friends. But they didn't allow these setbacks to dissolve their fellowship. Instead, they leaned into Jesus and each other. This resilience is the stuff of an authentic Christian community.

In his book, *The Coddling of the American Mind*, Jonathan Haidt discusses the positive effects of persisting in challenging environments:

---

[38] Dietrich Bonhoeffer, *Life Together: The Classic Exploration of Christian Community* (United Kingdom: HarperCollins, 2009), 27.

Some, like china teacups, are fragile: they break easily and cannot heal themselves, so you must handle them gently and keep them away from toddlers. Other things are resilient: they can withstand shocks. Parents usually give their toddlers plastic cups precisely because plastic can survive repeated falls to the floor, although the cups do not benefit from such falls. But we should look beyond the overused word "resilience" and recognize that some things are antifragile. Many of the important systems in our economic and political life are like our immune systems: they require stressors and challenges in order to learn, adapt, and grow. Systems that are antifragile become rigid, weak, and inefficient when nothing challenges them or pushes them to respond vigorously. He notes that muscles, bones, and children are antifragile.[39]

Haidt's term, antifragile, is an apt description for Christians who walk through fire and come out refined (Jas 1:2-3).

ACCEPT LIMITATIONS

FOMO ("fear of missing out") makes us reluctant to fully commit to a particular community. The fear of missing out means we always want to keep our options open, just in case. My oldest son tells me his friends are terrified of commitment, ever-ready to jump ship for something better. I don't

---

[39] Greg Lukianoff and Jonathan Haidt, *The Coddling of the American Mind: How Good Intentions and Bad Ideas Are Setting Up a Generation for Failure,* (United States: Penguin Publishing Group, 2019), 23.

think this problem is limited to twenty-somethings. The thing beneath the thing in our FOMO is a fear of monotony. We are addicted to novelty. In the words of John Steinbeck, we have an incurable "virus of restlessness."[40] The irony is, the deepest community is created by delighting in ordinary routines. Close families often have family traditions. Intimate marriages usually establish consistent rhythms. Healthy churches embrace liturgies that draw people toward Christ and each other. While adults dread monotony, children model what it looks like to delight in it, as G.K Chesterton beautifully observes:

> *Because children have abounding vitality, because they are in spirit fierce and free, therefore they want things repeated and unchanged. They always say, "Do it again"; and the grown-up person does it again until he is nearly dead. For grown-up people are not strong enough to exult in monotony. But perhaps God is strong enough to exult in monotony. It is possible that God says every morning, "Do it again" to the sun; and every evening, "Do it again" to the moon. It may not be an automatic necessity that makes all daisies alike, it may be that God makes every daisy separately, but he has never got tired of making them. It may be that He has the eternal appetite of*

---

[40] John Steinbeck, *Travels With Charley: In Search of America* (United Kingdom: Penguin Publishing Group, 1980), 3.

infancy; for we have sinned and grown old, and our Father is younger than we.[41]

As we abandon our fear of monotony to live alongside one another, we discover that Jesus infuses ordinary interactions with extraordinary grace.

OPEN YOUR LIFE

Finally, committing to a local community means opening our lives to others. It means sharing honestly about the state of our souls. Instead of wearing masks, we show our true selves.

There is such relief in bringing our souls out of the shadows into the light, where we realize we are not alone. 1 John 1:7 says, "But if we walk in the light, as he is in the light, we have fellowship with one another, and the blood of Jesus his Son cleanses us from all sin." When we confess our sins and struggles, instead of rejection we find deep fellowship with fellow saints who carry our burdens. True fellowship flows from true confession as the light of Christ chases our shadows away. It is a gift that halves our burdens and doubles our joys.

---

[41] G.K. Chesterton, *Orthodoxy* (United Kingdom: Lane, 1909), 108.

God has created you for community. You and I are de-signed to enjoy the presence of God dwelling among the people of God. Praising God in the midst of the festive throng does not have to be a distant memory. He invites you to join the joyful procession to the house of God once again. He invites you to reconnect your soul.

CHAPTER 7:
REFRESH YOUR SOUL

Deep calls to deep at the roar of your waterfalls;
All your breakers and your waves have gone over me.
By day the Lord commands his steadfast love,
and at night his song is with me, a prayer to the God of my life.
Psalm 42:7-8

As we've seen, Psalm 42 takes us on a journey from desperate thirst to deep refreshing. This Son of Korah (the author) begins by panting for streams of God's presence, but ends satisfied in him. His soul was cast down, but now plunges into a waterfall of God's love. His enemy-inflicted wounds have been healed by God-inspired wonder.

Psalm 42 illustrates how God is able to do more than we can ask or imagine (Eph 3:20), but that does not mean passivity on our part. There are no shortcuts to emotional health. Thankfully, this psalm does provide some formational clues to help guide us (pouring out your soul and speaking to your soul). Having explored these themes in previous chapters, I want to spend the closing chapter recommending some postures and practices that will help you plunge deeper into God's refreshing presence.

#1: INHABIT GOD'S WORD

If we are to plunge deeply into God's refreshing presence, we must own this psalm for ourselves. Of course, the first step is to understand the psalm in its original context before looking for personal application. It can't mean something to us that it didn't mean to them. But Psalm 42 isn't a theological relic from ancient Israel. It's meant for every generation of the church, including you and me. Thus, to read it theologically but not personally is to miss part of God's purpose in preserving this psalm in scripture. The Psalms don't merely aim to inform; they also transform.

Saint Augustine reasoned that, because the exact background situation of Psalm 42 is unknown, it allows Christians of all ages to apply it to their own lives more easily. Looking at the heartfelt words of Psalm 42, he writes:

Who says this? It is ourselves if we are willing. Such longing is not found in all who enter the Church; let all who have tasted the sweetness of the Lord and who relish Christ say: as the deer pants for streams of living water so my soul longs for you.[42]

Over the years, when my soul has been heavy with gloom or worry, I return to this psalm as a sacred conversation starter with God. It is not only the Son of Korah pouring out his soul to God, it is me, the son of Peter (my father), pouring his soul out, casting every care upon Jesus. I make his lament my own. I use his questions to listen to my soul. I borrow his hope to speak to my soul, reminding myself of the unchanging goodness of his God, who is also my God. I remind myself that God placed this psalm in his Book for a soul like mine. As I allow it to frame my prayer, it acts like a trellis to the vine of my soul, training it towards God's light, and I feel God's life returning. This psalm and this life are yours too, if you are willing.

#2: RECEIVE GOD'S GRACE

I have long been intrigued with the poetry of verse seven: "Deep calls to deep at the roar of your waterfalls." What

---

[42] Quoted in Carmen Joy Imes, *Praying the Psalms with Augustine and Friends* (United States: Sacred Roots, 2021), 82.

does it mean? At the very least, it means that there is no place in your soul so deep that God cannot speak to it. There's no crevice so dark that God cannot shine into it. To God, our depths are shallow and our darkness is light (Ps 139:12). I want you to think about the deepest, darkest place in your soul — the part that feels beyond God's redeeming reach. Tell your soul that God's steadfast love reaches even there.

Dane Ortlund, in his masterful book, *Gentle and Lowly*, writes:

> *We all tend to have some small pocket of our life where we have difficulty believing the forgiveness of God reaches. We say we are totally forgiven. And we sincerely believe our sins are forgiven. Pretty much, anyway. But there's that one deep, dark part of our lives, even our present lives, that seems so intractable, so ugly, so beyond recovery. "To the uttermost" in Hebrews 7:25 means: God's forgiving, redeeming, restoring touch reaches down into the darkest crevices of our souls, those places where we are most ashamed, most defeated. More than this: those crevices of sin are themselves the places where Christ loves us the most. His heart willingly goes there. His heart is most strongly drawn there. He knows us to the uttermost, and he saves us to the uttermost, because his heart is drawn out to us to the uttermost. We cannot sin our way out of his tender care.*[43]

---

[43] Dane Ortlund, *Gentle & Lowly: The Heart of Christ for Sinners and Sufferers* (United States: Crossway, 2020), 83.

Will you believe that God's deep love can speak to your deep longings? Will you trust that though your sin is deep, God's unfathomable grace is deeper still?

#3: ENJOY GOD'S GIFTS

The third posture is to be able to recognize and receive God's common grace for our soul's refreshing. We tend to overlook the good gifts of creation if we are overly mystical. This mindset is similar to first-century Gnosticism, a system of thought that denied the goodness of the material world. It was one of the chief heresies that threatened the early church as it denied the full humanity of Christ. Gnosticism doesn't recognize God's presence in common graces like nature, art, food, drink, sleep, sexual intimacy or physical exercise.

But God is certainly not a Gnostic. After creating the physical world, he called it good. Jesus, the Son of God, took on flesh and dwelt among us, learned a trade, spoke multiple languages, and was raised with a human body — all indicators that God values the embodied world. It's stunning to realize that those who are in Christ will be raised not only to a new heaven but also a new earth, where we will enjoy the fullness of God's creation, finally unleashed from the bonds of sin (Rom 8:20-21).

One of my favorite passages about God's common grace is the one in which Elijah flees after defeating the prophets of Baal. After a resounding victory by God's power, Elijah crashes into a pit of depression. You might expect God to scold Elijah, or tell him to perk up, but instead an angel of the Lord refreshes him with food and drink, then tells him to take a nap! He's commanded to do this twice. Elijah's exhaustion affects his emotions, and it's only after Elijah has been physically refreshed that he is able to hear God's voice clearly (1 Kings 19:13).

What practically fills your tank? What aesthetic setting aids you in connecting to the presence of God? I used to feel embarrassed that I take the same sea-green mug, make the same double shot flat white, and drink it in the same old leather chair each morning. I felt self-conscious that these little comforts helped my soul connect with the eternal God. Was I idolizing my environment or routine?

I've realized that I don't need to be embarrassed, because God created me with taste buds and a love for aesthetics. When I delight in those things, he is glorified. By the way, I love the fun fact that the spread of coffee across Europe co-incided with the spread of the gospel in the Reformation. Coffee does seem to be a special common grace!

I recently read a study about students who went through a period of doubt in their Christian faith. The decisive difference between those who emerged with their faith intact and those who deconverted was quite startling. Those who deconverted predominantly lived in cities while those who found resolution to their doubts lived in rural contexts. The researcher concluded that access to nature is a vital way people stay connected to their Creator. The lesson is not necessarily to move to the country, but it does speak to the necessity of enjoying God's creation regularly.

I've experienced God's refreshing presence in ordinary ways: with friends around a meat smoker, watching whales frolic in the Pacific, in the pages of a classic novel, and on a candle-lit marriage bed. These moments may seem less "spiritual" than morning devotions or gathered worship, but they're no less sacred. As Abraham Kuyper famously declared: "There is not a square inch in the whole domain of our human existence over which Christ, who is Sovereign over all, does not cry: 'Mine!'"[44]

---

[44] Abraham Kuyper, "Sphere Sovereignty". Found in https://media.thegospelcoalition.org/wp-content/uploads/2017/06/24130543/SphereSovereignty_English.pdf

Kuyper was merely echoing King David's sentiment in the Psalms: "The earth is the Lord's and the fulness thereof" (Ps 24:1). The Lord has given us the gift of his creation in order to communicate his goodness to us. It is a happy discipline of God's children to acknowledge the sacred in the ordinary.

HOPE FOR THE SATURATED SOUL

I pray the practices above are helpful, and while this book seeks to provide a formational process for healing our saturated souls, our ultimate hope isn't in a process — it's in a Person. Tangible steps can benefit us, but only when done with Christ.

This is why I love Psalm 23, which describes Jesus as our Good Shepherd. In the New Testament, the Greek word for "shepherd" is *poimein*, which means "to guard and to care for." Like a sheep lost and tattered in the wilderness, to be healed we need someone to lead us to safety. The author is King David, who was highly familiar with sheep from his boyhood years as a shepherd. He speaks of God as his shepherd, who restores his soul by leading him beside still waters. No good shepherd leaves his sheep to starve of thirst or get shredded by ravenous wolves. Thus, along with David, we need not fear deep valleys of darkness. For it is there, not on the mountaintops, that refreshing streams flow. Our Good Shepherd promises we will be refreshed and well-watered, even though sometimes we have to sojourn through treacherous terrain. In the deepest valleys Christ leads us to the freshest rivers.

LET THE THIRSTY DRINK

John's gospel, more than any other, explains that Jesus is the Good Shepherd of Psalm 23. In John 10:11, Jesus claims to fulfill this role explicitly: "I am the Good Shepherd. The Good Shepherd lays down his life for the sheep." Jesus, the Good Shepherd lays down his life like a sacrificial lamb to take away the sins of the world.

Like the shepherd in Psalm 23, Jesus leads his flock to still waters so they can be refreshed. John records a poignant moment in Jesus' ministry to illustrate this, when at the Feast of Booths he stands up and declares:

> *"If anyone thirsts, let him come to me and drink. Whoever believes in me, as the Scripture has said, 'Out of his heart will flow rivers of living water.'" Now this he said about the Spirit, whom those who believed in him were to receive, for as yet the Spirit had not been given, because Jesus was not yet glorified.*
> John 7:37-39

Jesus promised that after he was crucified, raised on the third day and glorified in his ascension, he would pour out his Spirit on those who believed in him. This promise was foretold by the prophet Joel, "In the last days I will pour out my Spirit on all flesh…" (Joel 2:14), and fulfilled at Pentecost when the church was born and baptized in the Spirit (Acts 2:1-39). This is why Ephesians 5:18 commands all believers to "not get drunk with wine but be filled with the Spirit." The apostle Paul gives this command in the present tense, which indicates ongoing, continuous action. In a very real sense he is saying, "Be *continuously* filled with the Spirit." Let's not get caught up in debates about whether baptism in the Spirit is simultaneous with salvation or subsequent to being saved. The truth is that the Holy Spirit indwells every believer, but this is not the same as being filled with the Spirit. This Spirit infilling is a continuous invitation to drink deeply of God's presence, which heals us, restores us, and overflows our souls with joy.

Jesus saves us from sin and heals our wounds, but beyond all that he also satisfies our souls. When we've tasted his goodness, cracked cisterns no longer satisfy! May the Good Shepherd restore your soul, plunging you into the refreshing waterwall of his Spirit. You are his, and nothing can snatch you out of his hand.

BIBLIOGRAPHY

Baker, Ken. *Our Father: Living the Lord's Prayer.* N.p.: Lulu.com, 2017.

Bonhoeffer, Dietrich. *Life Together: The Classic Exploration of Christian Community.* United Kingdom: HarperCollins, 2009.

Bonhoeffer, Dietrich. *Life Together and Prayerbook of the Bible* (vol. 5 of Dietrich Bonhoeffer Works). Minneapolis: Fortress Press, 1996.

Brueggemann, Walter. *Praying the Psalms: Engaging Scripture and the Life of the Spirit.* United States: Cascade Books, 2007.

Calvin, John. *Commentary on the Book of Psalms.* Vol. 1. Translated by James Anderson. Grand Rapids, MI: Christian Classics Ethereal Library, https://www.ccel.org/ccel/calvin/calcom08/calcom08.i.html

Carson, D. A.. *For the Love of God: A Daily Companion for Discovering the Riches of God's Word.* Volume 1. United States: Crossway, 2006.

Chesterton, G.K. *Orthodoxy.* United Kingdom: Lane, 1909.

Critchley, Robert. "My Hope is Built on Nothing Less." Musixmatch, 2007. Accessed March 9, 2022. https://www.musixmatch.com/lyrics/Robert-Critchley/My-Hope-Is-Built-on-Nothing-Less-On-Christ-The-Solid-Rock.

Dever, Mark. *The Message of the New Testament: Promises Kept.* United States: Crossway Books, 2005.

Earley, Dave, Gutiérrez, Ben. *Ministry Is . . ..* United States: B&H Publishing Group, 2010.

Edgar, William. *Created and Creating: A Biblical Theology of Culture.* United States: InterVarsity Press, 2016.

Franklin, Benjamin, Gutmann, Amy. *The Autobiography of Benjamin Franklin.* Penn Reading Project Edition. Ukraine: University of Pennsylvania Press, Incorporated, 2010.

Imes, Carmen Joy. *Praying the Psalms with Augustine and Friends.* United States: Sacred Roots, 2021.

Ingham, Michael. *Rites for a New Age: Understanding the Book of Alternative Services.* Canada: Anglican Book Center, 1986.

Jones, Tony. "Darrin Patrick: 'There's Something about the Woods.'" The Reverend Hunter Podcast, May 18, 2020, https://podcasts.apple.com/us/podcast/darrin-patrick-theres-something-about-the-woods/id1500247799?i=1000474969379

Keller, Kathy. "The Dangers of Faking it in Ministry." The Gospel Coalition, Feb. 14, 2013, https://www.thegospelcoalition.org/article/the-dangers-of-faking-it-in-ministry.

Keller, Timothy. *Prayer: Experiencing Awe and Intimacy with God.* United States: Penguin Publishing Group, 2014.

Kris, Deborah Farmer. "What's Mentionable is Manageable: Why Parents Should Help Children Name their Fears." *The Washington Post,* Sept. 20, 2018. https://www.washingtonpost.com/news/Parenting/wp/2018/09/20/whats-mentionable-is-manageable-why-parents-should-help-kids-name-their-fears.

Lewis, C.S. *Mere Christianity.* New York: Macmillan, 1952.

Lewis, C.S. *Reflections on the Psalms.* United Kingdom: Harcourt, Brace, 1958.

Lewis, C. S. *The Four Loves*. United Kingdom: HarperCollins Publishers, 2010.

Lewis, C. S. *The Screwtape Letters*. South Korea: HarperCollins, 2001.

Lloyd-Jones, D. Martyn. *Spiritual Depression: Its Causes and Cure*. United States: Eerdmans Publishing Company, 1965.

Lukianoff, Greg, Haidt, Jonathan. *The Coddling of the American Mind: How Good Intentions and Bad Ideas Are Setting Up a Generation for Failure*. United States: Penguin Publishing Group, 2019.

Manning, Brennan. *The Ragamuffin Gospel*. United States: Multnomah Books, 2015.

Nouwen, Henri. *The Return of the Prodigal Son: A Story of Homecoming*. United States: Crown Publishing Group, 2013.

Ortlund, Dane. *Gentle and Lowly: The Heart of Christ for Sinners and Sufferers*. United States: Crossway, 2020.

Peterson, Andrew. "Is He Worthy?" Genius. Accessed March 10, 2002. https://genius.com/Andrew-peterson-is-he-worthy-lyrics

Pink Floyd. "Comfortably Numb." Genius. Accessed April 4, 2022.https://genius.com/Pink-floyd-comfortably-numb-lyrics.

"Poisonous Plants of Belize & Central America." Consejo Belize. Accessed March 28, 2022. http://consejo.bz/belize/ poison-plants/poisonplants.html.

Rascal Flatts. "I Feel Bad." Genius. Accessed April 4, 2022. https://genius.com/Rascal-flatts-i-feel-bad-lyrics

Scazzero, Peter. *Emotionally Healthy Spirituality: It's Impossible to Be Spiritually Mature, While Remaining Emotionally Immature*. United States: Zondervan, 2017.

"Self-Injury/ Cutting." Mayo Clinic. Dec. 7, 2018. https://www.mayoclinic.org/diseases-conditions/self-injury/symptoms-causes/syc-20350950

Shakespeare, William. Hamlet, *The Prince of Denmark*. Open Source Shakespeare. United States: George Mason University, 2003, 1.3.565.https://www.opensourceshakespeare.org/views/plays /play_view.php?Act=1&Scene=3&Scope=scene&WorkID=h amlet

Steinbeck, John. *Travels With Charley: In Search of America*. United Kingdom: Penguin Publishing Group, 1980.

Stott, John. *I Believe in Preaching*. United Kingdom: Hodder & Stoughton, 2014.

Swift, Taylor. "Bad Blood." Genius, 2014. Accessed March 11, 2002. https://genius.com/Taylor-swift-bad-blood-lyrics.

Tripp, Paul David. *New Morning Mercies: A Daily Gospel Devotional*. United States: Crossway, 2014.

U2. "God Part II." Genius, 1998. Accessed March 10, 2002. https://genius.com/U2-god-part-ii-lyrics.

Warren, Tish Harrison. "How a Cancer Diagnosis Makes Jesus' Death and Resurrection Mean More." New York Times, April 10, 2022. https://www.nytimes.com/2022/04/10/opinion/ timothy-keller-cancer-easter.html

Williamson, Marianne. "Forgiveness: Why Holding onto that Grudge Will Only Hurt You." Christianity Today, March 31, 2016.https://www.christiantoday.com/article/forgiveness.why .holding.onto.that.grudge.will.only.hurt.you/83008.htm